Education, Extremism and Terrorism

Also available from Continuum:

Education and Community, Dianne Gereluk
Education as a Global Concern, Colin Brock
Multiculturalism and Education, Richard Race
Symbolic Clothing in Schools, Dianne Gereluk
Teaching Citizenship Education, Ralph Leighton
Teaching Controversial Issues in the Classroom, Paula Cowan and Henry Maitles

Education, Extremism and Terrorism

What should be Taught in Citizenship Education and Why

DIANNE GERELUK

continuum

Continuum International Publishing Group

The Tower Building
11 York Road
London
SE1 7NX

80 Maiden Lane
Suite 704
New York
NY 10038

www.continuumbooks.com

British Library Cataloguing-in-Publication Data
A catalogue record for this book is available from the British Library.

ISBN: 978-1-4411-0515-8 (paperback)
978-1-4411-6971-6 (hardcover)
978-1-4411-2786-0 (ePub)
978-1-4411-5142-1 (PDF)

Library of Congress Cataloging-in-Publication Data
Gereluk, Dianne.
Education, extremism and terrorism : what should be taught in citizenship education and why / Dianne Gereluk.
p. cm.
Summary: "A thorough exploration of how the issues of extremism and terrorism should be addressed and taught in schools" – Provided by publisher.
Includes bibliographical references and index.
ISBN 978-1-4411-0515-8 (pbk) – ISBN 978-1-4411-6971-6 (hardcover) – ISBN 978-1-4411-2786-0 (ebook ePub) 1. Citizenship – Study and teaching. 2. Civics – Study and teaching. 3. Radicalism – Study and teaching. 4. Terrorism – Study and teaching. I. Title.
LC1091.G446 2012
372.89–dc23
2011036195

Typeset by Fakenham Prepress Solutions, Fakenham, Norfolk NR21 8NN
Printed and bound in India

To my mother,
Eileen Makowecki,
who embodies both a strong character
and kindness of heart.

CONTENTS

FOREWORD

Terror and terrorism are nothing new in human experience. Most of the world's population is confronted with terror in one form or another, in both visceral and psychological forms, as a matter of routine. Nature offers up myriad terrors: those of hurricane and drought, or malaria, cholera and AIDS. Human terrors, too, abound. Millions suffer the direct and indirect effects of civil war and genocide, including hidden psychological scars and persistent threats (e.g., landmines) inherited from the previous generation's fear and hatred. Sometimes Nature's fury combines with ruthless power to produce famine, extreme poverty and degradation, the state of desperation that is life-as-usual for innumerable wretched souls. For millions, terror is simply life itself.

But the invocation of extremism and terrorism for most of us conjures up particular images. We associate these terms with dramatic events. Perhaps most of us think of someone like Anders Breivik, who enacted a rampage of terror on innocent children at a summer camp, shattering the illusion of Scandinavian tranquillity. Or maybe we recall the Beslan school tragedy in which hundreds were killed following a hostage standoff with Russian military in North Ossetia. Or perhaps we reflect on *responses* to terror and violence: how the death of a Tunisian boy sparked a popular democratic revolution sweeping across north Africa, Syria and Yemen, a revolution that continues unabated. Repressive regimes, long supported by Western governments, have been overthrown while others continue to murder and terrorize their own citizens.

Terrorism is of course not restricted to non-democratic societies. Democratic India experiences more human terrorism than any country on earth. Some highly industrialised nations of east Asia are confronted not only with tsunamis and earthquakes but also with mass imprisonment and torture, not to mention encroaching religious extremism. Then there is Oklahoma City, New York,

Paris, Madrid, London, all metaphors in the lexicon of extremism and violence. Around the world on a smaller but no less dramatic scale there are rapes and killings in neighbourhoods and schools. No place is immune to extremism or violence.

There is a thin line separating unrest and violence from extremism. In the summer of 2011 the world watched as festering tensions erupted into violence on the streets of Britain over the police shooting of a young man. Extremist or not, the alleged cause of these events – no doubt shamelessly exploited by countless disenfranchised youth as well as the media – serves to remind us that all is not well. We should not be surprised. Fact is that any society, rent from top to bottom with socio-economic inequities, restricted liberties, ethnic and religious tensions, corrupt officials, and high levels of social segregation is a time bomb waiting to go off. There is in fact an unnerving predictability to social unrest and violence when social inequities and exclusion mark the lives of entire communities.

One-sided responses to unrest and violence are instructive. The Tory response was predictable enough, accusing individual actors of lawlessness – true enough – and to reduce the causes of the unrest to their own absence of a moral compass. But when the diagnosis of societal ills is parsimonious, other factors unavoidably are left unexamined – among them festering post-colonial racisms, police profiling and excessive force, a vanishing welfare state, and unprecedented levels of unemployment in the midst of an economic crisis. Of course these conditions are not isolated to Britain, as a pall continues to hang over the Euro zone and other nations tremble at the thought of partners defaulting on their loans. Structured to benefit some (e.g., large corporations and banks) while disadvantaging or excluding many others, the indiscriminate ebb and flow of investment capital threatens further instability. Hardly anyone is unaffected, though of course some are affected far more than others.

There is anger, fear, confusion and vulnerability on all sides. Given these fears and the ease with which information, cargo and persons now travel, unprecedented levels of security now pervade daily life: 24 hour video surveillance, body scanners, computer filtering systems, and of course intelligence gathering agencies operating carte blanche as they tap our phones and rifle through private information to which they have virtually unlimited access.

Each of these tactics, invariably justified in the interest of public safety, attempts to prevent but not understand underlying causes of extremism. Other time bombs await: in north-western continental Europe small welfare states, whose immigration policies are among the strictest in the world, placate their own disenfranchised minorities and poor with basic incomes, housing and health insurance. Providing refugees, immigrants and asylum seekers with subsidized housing and health care certainly helps to dampen violent impulses but it does very little to make one feel welcome. 'Integration' is on everyone's lips, but the psychological underpinnings of integration are missing. In its place familiar oppositional thinking – us and them – is commonplace.

So how should we talk about violence and extremism? How might individuals and groups be identified and discussed without lapsing into stereotype and blame games? How might society be organized differently to lessen the possibility of extremism and violence in the first place? Will shared values and norms help to promote a feeling of belonging, and will that feeling be widely shared by others? What is needed to promote that connectedness? What should the school's role be in all this? How ought textbooks, teachers and parents respond to such sensitive issues of extremism and violence, particularly when they affect the lives of young children? Framing her discussion around basic principles of justice, Gereluk's book fearlessly tackles many of these and many other timely questions and invites teachers and students alike to think along.

Michael S. Merry, University of Amsterdam

ACKNOWLEDGEMENTS

My impetus for writing any book usually evolves in the same way. In the beginning, a germinating idea emerges slowly as an unresolved tension, an ambiguity, or a perplexing issue. It is unclear how the idea will develop or whether this pause warrants further discussion or exploration. And inevitably, the idea resonates with so many others that in the end one wonders where one person's idea begins and another's continues on. And so, here I find myself, once again in wonderment with what started as a personal uncomfortable stance with the aftermath of 9/11 and 7/7 and the educational implications of how to address these events, and similar responses and reactions by other colleagues who were grappling with how to address them within their own areas of expertise.

I am very grateful for the mentorship and guidance of Professor Ron Best and Dr. Richard Race, who initiated a series of conversations with me about the implications and aftermath of 9/11 and 7/7 for schools and higher education. Ron Best had a particular interest in the personal, social, health education (PSHE) curriculum of study that is taught in the United Kingdom, and found himself wondering how the terrorist events would affect individuals' sense of care and emotional well-being. Richard Race examined the political change from multiculturalism to 'Britishness' and considered how civil society should be organized, particularly given the changing tone from multiculturalism to that of developing social cohesion through a British national identity. I found myself again considering the parameters of religious and cultural accommodation within civil society given the perception of increased extremist fundamentalism and terrorism locally and abroad. As such, we found our paths crossing and came together to organize a conference on 'Education and Extremism' to bring together other academics who were also grappling with the subject matter. This initial conference gave me the support and excitement to embark on a larger book project to explore the issue in more depth. I thank you both for your support and shared experiences.

Many thanks to Alexandra Xanthaki who first showed me a list of numerous news clippings from leading national newspapers, highlighting the increased fear and anxiety that followed the 7/7 terrorist attacks in London. The heightened panic and media attention alerted me for the need to develop these ideas further after the Education and Extremism conference that was held in summer 2007.

Cheryl Sawyer kindly agreed to give me permission to reprint her poem, 'One'. Her conversations regarding how to deal with trauma with children in schools proved most enlightening, with regard not only to political trauma, but also to other forms of crisis such as natural disasters and economic crises. She confirmed some of my suspicions regarding the reluctance of schools to address these crises given their sensitive and controversial nature from a counselling perspective. The struggles of discussing difficult topics in the classroom – in her line of counselling, to that of my area in educational policy – was both illuminating and disconcerting at the same time.

My work with other colleagues on philosophical principles regarding how sensitive controversial topics should be addressed in schools helped me to consider how one might broach this particular topic. My fellow colleagues Michael Hand, Paula McAvoy, Bryan Warnick, Sigal Ben-Porath, Leonard Waks, Richard Bailey, Patricia White, Kevin McDonough, Lynn Bosetti, Yvonne Hébert, and Kent Donlevy have all given me the proper encouragement and support through this research project. You have said the 'right' things at the right time, particularly when I was making a transition in my career from an academic in England to one in Canada.

My online community participated in many debates and discussions when I posed a question regarding how educators might broach the topic of extremism and terrorism, and my request to 'name your favourite villain' movie elicited over 60 replies in under half an hour. It was both fascinating and shocking to see how individuals could rattle off their favourite enemy. So to my friends online, who obviously watch more movies than I could imagine, I thank you for your enthused debates and dialogues.

Each time I decide to write a book, it comes with a cost to those dear to me. So, to my children, Katya and Roman, thank you for providing your endless smiles and cuddles, your much needed play times and story breaks. Your love carried me through many a weak moment when I was both tired and grumpy. To my husband Marlow, thank you for believing in me.

Introduction

I can remember the day when the planes hit the World Trade Center. I was in my home in central London working on my PhD dissertation. I had no TV, but spent a lot of time instant messaging my friends as I slowly plodded along writing a few words toward the finished product. My fellow classmate, an American, sent me a text and asked me if I had seen what was happening. I hadn't, and my initial thoughts were that the first reports of a plane hitting the first building were that of pilot error. The second plane that hit the building seemed like a hoax. Reality set in when my husband called and said that he had to leave the financial district in central London for fear of similar attacks occurring there.

The next few days were a blur. Friends who had planned to 'spend the night' before heading on a flight back home to Canada found themselves in limbo in London waiting for the 'no fly' zone to be lifted. Other American friends had planned their honeymoon in Turkey shortly following the attacks, and resolved to continue with their plans, to the fear and cajoling of friends and family. (They were fine, and had a lovely time.)

Why was this event so significant? Only a year prior to 9/11, two terrorist bombs had been detonated within a few kilometres of my residence in London by the IRA, and people took it in their stride as part of the hazards of living in London. The bombings of 7/7 in London in 2005 provoked a similar shock to that of 9/11. As academics, we were now asked to watch out for extremist tendencies or unusual behaviour among our students and report it to the authorities. A lecture that I gave regularly to my undergraduate students was on the promotion of multiculturalism and diversity in education. Now the tone of the lecture had shifted to include the possibility that 'multiculturalism was dead' and 'social cohesion/assimilation' was in. And somewhere in the middle, schools would need to ignore the elephant in the room – that of extremist fundamentalism or terrorism – often teachers feeling incredibly ill-prepared to discuss the issue. Commonly, teachers expressed that they had addressed the topic inadequately and even inappropriately. Conflicting and patchy guidance did not help the matter further. Teacher education programmes continued to train teachers with little interruption to consider how a teacher might broach the topic of extremism and terrorism.

A number of my colleagues grappled with how to address the issues of extremism and terrorism appropriately in our schools and universities; for the most part, many of us did not attempt to introduce the topic in our lectures, but confined discussions to an informal level in offices or during breaks. These initial conversations, however, created a need to elevate the discussion to a more formal examination of how one should address extremism and terrorism. Our attempts to develop a provocative yet open title for our conference elicited complaints from other colleagues who thought that we had targeted Muslim communities and called to ban the title of the proposed conference: 'What should we teach about terrorism?'(Gereluk et al., 2007a). The reasons for such objection to the title were stated as follows:[1]

1. In the present climate, *'terrorism'* and *'war on terrorism'* have direct association with the Muslim community and to use such wording in a conference title implies the same connections and is therefore insensitive. While the wording may wish to be deliberately controversial, it should not do so at the expense of being offensive, particularly if you wish to engage in dialogue with members of the community you are offending.

2. There are some ill-chosen linkages in the text that would not be expected from a group that is claiming to seek detached discourse in this area:

   ● Northern Ireland, terrorism and faith schools

   ● 9/11, 7/7 and teachers in Faith community schools

---

[1] The following passages are taken from a paper that was presented at the British Education Research Association, pp. 1–4 (Best et al., 2007a).

- 'rational debate' and emotive headlining.

3. 'Borat' syndrome: the tone and language of the discussion so far has more of a feel of 'Borat' about it than an invitation to participate in a detached and informed academic discourse.

4. An alternative title:

even though the linkage or juxtaposition of many of these issues may be judged inappropriate, many of them are worthy of open and public discourse that a conference could provide. In support, therefore, we offer some alternative titles for such a conference:

- Religion, Citizenship and Globalisation

- Fervour, Fundamentalism, Fanaticism and Freedom

- Religious Identity in Geo-Politics

- Faith Community Schools and Social Cohesion.

(*ibid.*, p. 3)

It is instructive to analyse in some depth what the objections were to the proposal which the planning team made.

First, the objections were primarily to do with the title, and here the bogey word was *terrorism*. As noted above, the compromise at the highest levels was that 'extremism' might be substituted for 'terrorism' in the title, and those with the power would not be drawn by an attempt to reinstate it through the use of a subtitle. In the e-mail attachment from colleagues, the initial objection is based on the fact that 'in the present climate [this word, and its relatives such as "war on terror"] have direct association with the Muslim community'. They go on to say that to use these words is to imply 'the same connections'.

What is the 'climate' to which they refer? Commonly, individuals talk of the 'climate of opinion', the 'political climate', 'climate of fear', the 'current economic climate' and so on. Presumably, the objectors are referring to the political climate, the climate of opinion or, perhaps, a climate of beliefs. If so, it is pertinent to ask where these opinions, ideas or beliefs are to be observed. They may well be observed in the pubs and shopping centres, the parlours and dining rooms and the parks and street corners of this society, but they are very much more to be observed in the mass media. We would not have the phrase 'war on terror' in everyday conversation if the media had not reported the words of the politicians, notably Bush and Blair, and had not presented the news in similar terms. And it may well be the case that these words cannot now be used without evoking some of the connections that were explicit or implicit in what those politicians said. But it would be entirely fallacious to assume that to use these words is necessarily to endorse the validity of those connections, or that their use is inescapably offensive to groups or individuals. This surely depends upon the context within which they are used.

In the second paragraph, 'ill-chosen linkages' are alleged: those between issues or events which a conference aimed at 'detached discourse' would not so link. Here, too, the nub of the matter is that there are connections (here 'linkages') which are apparently objectionable. To juxtapose certain words or to use them in certain combinations may well be a ploy by which to insinuate, more or less subtly, certain value positions into a conversation or dialogue, and we may infer that this is what the objectors felt the team to be doing. But what would a 'detached' discourse be like? On one meaning of the word, a discourse necessarily has an element of power within it: it is about what can and cannot be admitted to a conversation and thus about who *says* what is admissible. In this sense, a 'detached' discourse would be impossible. A discourse is not to be confused with a *dialogue* or a *debate* (which is probably what the objectors really meant).

The third objection is an interesting example of the power of the media in determining the vocabulary in which arguments can take place; it presupposes familiarity with a particular media 'event' or 'document' in order to deride a proposal for a totally dissimilar event or document (a conference).

Finally, despite the contested words 'associations' and 'linkages' above, the objectors consider that 'many of [the issues] are worthy of open and public discourse' [by which they probably mean dialogue, debate or discussion], and they offer some alternative titles. It is unclear in what ways these formulations might be thought to be 'as good as', let alone 'better' than, the original proposal. In so far as none of these words has the same literal meaning, common etymology or current nuances as 'terrorism', it is difficult to see how they could convey the same meaning with regard to the concerns that motivated the conference planning team. The conference would, inevitably, be about something other than terrorism, since what is unique in the meaning of the word 'terrorism' cannot be present without using that word. Moreover, to be consistent, a case would have to be made to the effect that none of these formulations involved 'juxtapositions', 'associations' or 'linkages' that would resonate with existing 'climates' and thus likely to be 'offensive' to any social group.

Taken together, the objections raised amount to a concession that the issue was worthy of debate but an insistence that the topic could not be named and could not be debated in the only language that could do it justice. It might only be discussed, it seems, in euphemisms which, by definition, could at best refer obliquely to what we the conference proposers were really on about. They might have a conference, but the conference dare not speak its name.

The 'tyranny' of language is that in order to utter and communicate ideas, we *must* use words, and as expressions of shared symbolic universes, the meanings at our disposal are necessarily limited by the words available to us. When we struggle to express a new idea, we struggle precisely because we need new words (or new combinations of words) to express the hitherto unexpressed or inexpressible. To proscribe certain linguistic forms and to prescribe others – to lay down the law about what words we may or may not use – is the behaviour of the tyrant; it says (in effect): I control your thoughts by controlling the language you are free to use. Ironically, the objectors in this case attempted to exercise this kind of control by denying the conference organizers the right to use the language of the current 'war on terror' in order to engage with the misconceptions, innuendos and offensive associations it entails. The ultimate outcome of such a policy is not unlike the conspiracy to conceal the truth about the emperor's new clothes: a failure to challenge is to permit the lie to continue.

Despite the debate that ensued among the committee and their colleagues who found the conference title offensive, the committee were advised that if no amendments to the title of the conference were made, the promised internal funding would be withdrawn. The response was that although the conference had support at the highest level, it would be helpful to 'lower the temperature with colleagues' if possible, and that *Education and Extremism* was considered to be 'a good title'. A request for permission to use the subtitle *Towards a rational approach to terrorism* received a non-committal response.

While the conference did eventually gain approval under a different title, 'Extremism and Education', the highly contested and volatile situation is worthy to note. What is significant from the objections is the emotive response regarding the nature of the language, and the politics of higher education institutions and the potential curtailment of academic freedom and scholarly activity in universities. While the circumstances surrounding this particular anecdote may be unique, many other academics found themselves under greater surveillance following 9/11 and 7/7 (Carvalho and Downing, 2010). While in times of calm, academic freedom is considered fundamental to the preservation of original thought and research. Yet, in times of perceived crisis, the reins are drawn in and mechanisms are put in place to restrain academics under the discourse of national security. Tenure has been revoked and teaching positions have been closed since 9/11.

> Some of the more virulent witch hunts in the post-9/11 university are those experienced by the likes of Sami Al-Arian, Norman Finelstein, Joseph Massad, Nadia Abu El-Haj, Tariq Ramadan (and, most recently, Joel Kovel, Margo Ramlal-Nankoe, and William Robinson) most of whom have published and lectured widely on the realities of the Israeli-occupied territories and Palestinian suffering.
>
> (*ibid.*, pp. 10–11)

While academic research and teaching practices are under greater scrutiny, students are facing similar tighter controls. Fewer international student applications were received by higher educational institutions and even fewer were approved in the United States after 9/11 as a result of heightened security measures to attain student visas and for fear of bringing in potential extremist behaviours to their campus.

The fear and anxiety of 9/11 and 7/7 have created a chill in what can and cannot be said, who can be admitted, and how one should proceed. Yet, as my colleagues and I have argued before (Gereluk et al., 2007), it is precisely a conscious and deliberate conversation that is required in understanding and examining how one might address terrorism and extremism. So let us begin by considering what is meant by extremism and terrorism before we consider how we might address it in schools.

Terms regarding extremism and terrorism

The way in which language evokes such strong sentiments as illustrated above suggests that a pause is required to consider the ways in which 'extremism' and terrorism' are used and understood. It is important to make distinctions between the notions of extremism and terrorism before we move into the heart of the debates.

Extremism in its broadest sense is an individual or group of individuals who take an extreme position from that of the norm, or take an extreme action. Commonly, those with extremist perspectives have a particular perspective or belief 'in the sense that they take their opinions or beliefs to the limit and do not allow much room for the existence of any other views of life' (Zarabozo, 2003, p. 51). Notions of extremism vary in its emphases, but overlapping principles come into play when individuals attempt to define extremism:

1. Location at a corner rather than in the interior of some dimension of individual's preferences. Sometimes, relatedly, extremism is defined as moving away from the center towards the extreme rather than an equilibrium position;

2. A characteristic of the way beliefs are held rather their location in some dimension; for example if they are held rigidly or the person holding them displays a small capacity or willingness to compromise;

3. A shrinking of the range, or a limitation of the number of options and choices which are considered;

4. The salience or importance of belief or set of beliefs; that is, an extremist who is fixated on some idea or belief;

5. The means used; for example, a political extremist is one who resorts to terror or violence to further political ends.
(Breton et al., 2002, p. xiii)

Although these points attend to different emphases, a common overlapping principle is that an extremist is one who has a particular perspective to the exclusion of other perspectives or that it strays from the accepted norms and behaviours of mainstream society.

Terrorism is the violent act or event against innocent individuals to incite fear or anxiety among a citizenry. So, for example, we might suggest that the views of an individual that go beyond the parameters of the norm or behaviours of most in society might be perceived as having an extremist view or position. The physical doing of something to elicit fear among the general public might be considered that of 'terrorism'. Debates arise whether violence carried out by government or non-government constitutes that of terrorism. Other rhetorical devices are used to contest the definition of terrorism whether 'one person's terrorist is another person's freedom fighter' depending on the motive that gives rise to violent acts (Laqueur, 1987, pp. 7, 302). Goax Bonar (2002) offers a straight-forward and clear definition that is useful for how we consider what constitutes terrorism. Three main principles provide guidance for how we can move beyond the semantic arguments surrounding terrorism. Bonar posits the following:

1. The essence of the activity – the use of, or threat to use, violence. According to this definition, an activity that does not involve violence or a threat of violence will not be defined as terrorism (including nonviolent protest – strikes, peaceful demonstrations, tax revolts, etc.).

2. The aim of the activity is always political – namely, the goal is to attain political objectives: changing the regime, changing the people in power, changing social or economic policies, etc.

3. The targets of terrorism are civilians. Terrorism is thus distinguished from other types of political violence (guerrilla warfare, civil insurrection, etc.). Terrorism exploits the relative vulnerability of the civilian 'underbelly' – the tremendous anxiety, and the intense media reaction evoked by attacks against civilian targets. The proposed definition emphasizes that terrorism is not the result of an accidental injury inflicted on a civilian or a group of civilians who stumbled into an area of violent political activity, but stresses that this is an act purposely directed against civilians.

(*ibid.*, pp. 293–4)

These three simple yet powerful principles offer a way in which to make distinctions for how one might proceed and distinguish terrorism from that of other violent acts or forms of military intervention. I use both these definitions of extremism and terrorism as my starting point for this book. While individuals may wish to challenge these definitions, I wish to move forth in how schools might address these issues, rather than focus on such semantic debates. This is best left to linguists and political scientists.

Both terms connote normative values and elicit political responses. Bush's phrase, 'The War on Terror', for instance, was used to demonstrate that there was a clear direction to be taken – that of war – and was not for debate (Melnyk, 2010, p. 105). To suggest something other than a clear course for action following the 9/11 attacks in Congress would have shown gross disrespect and lack of patriotism for America. We might further solicit phrases of terrorism as being acts of 'evil'. The embedded political ideologies are notable and contested so much that the United Nations has come to little consensus of how to define 'terrorism'. Yet, it conjures an emotive response, something that is negative and elusive, scary and uncertain. The moral implications are that it is something to be avoided and curtailed at most costs. Louise Richardson (2007) succinctly states:

> The term [terrorism] has been bandied about so much that it has come to lose all meaning ... if you can successfully pin the label [terrorist] on your opponent you have gone a long way towards winning the public relations aspect of any conflict.
>
> (*ibid.*, p. 19)

In setting up this oppositional force between 'us' and 'them', the notions of terrorism then have implications for how educators might address topics in schools.[2] If the public's perception is to secure certain values in its fight against terrorism – 'national security', 'freedom', 'the public good' – should schools further or remain neutral regarding such values? The politically charged and moral weight of terrorism makes it a difficult tightrope for educators to negotiate.

---

[2] This will be addressed thoroughly in Chapter 3.

Conclusion

In the coming chapters, we will walk that fine tightrope, attempting to address some of the multiple and, at times, conflicting messages that schools are being asked to facilitate in their classrooms. As you read this book, I will ask you at various points to reflect on your own position throughout the discussion on the extent to which terrorism should be taught in schools, primarily related to 9/11 and 7/7 (although not exclusively). These will be marked in the 'Pause for thought' sections throughout this book. Part of the task will be for you to consider whether your views change as you progress through this debate or whether they stay the same. The second major task is whether you can provide some justifications to support the position that you have taken. The intent of the book is not to convince you of *my* opinion, but rather for you to enter into a deliberative dialogue. I may put forth a position, but you must negotiate the arguments presented and consider where you stand. The nature of the contested issues such as this will rarely (almost impossibly), achieve consensus. Yet, as a teacher, educator or leader, you will need to negotiate such difficult circumstances in the daily experiences you encounter in your own educational institution. It is clear that by the end of this book, we will reach little consensus, and perhaps I will evoke strong sentiments. At the very least, the fundamental aim of this book is to elucidate the complexity and contentious nature around the notions of 'extremism' and 'terrorism', both in how it has been taken up, and how we ought to proceed in a critically reflective and reasoned manner.

In what follows, I begin by introducing the reader to the debate regarding extremism and terrorism, particularly related to education. Particular reference would be made to media clippings and various educational responses to deal with the events following 9/11 and 7/7. I compare and contrast the ways in which the United States and the United Kingdom have attempted to address it in its multiple, and at times competing, ways. The British government has attempted to address this by implementing the 'Preventing Violent Extremism' agenda that includes a school toolkit, 'Learning Together to be Safe', to help schools address the prevention of violent extremism. In contrast, a number of various textbooks and supplementary curriculum materials have been written in the United States to address the events of 9/11 – mostly focusing on narrating the events with little competing interpretations and analyses. I highlight these varied approaches to set the foundation for some of the contested debates that arise when we consider what is at stake when addressing extremism and terrorism.

Chapter 2 considers how issues of terrorism and extremism might be broached in the classroom. This chapter explores and critiques various reasons why terrorism and extremism might be considered worthwhile topics to teach in schools. Such rationales may include: to develop a more cohesive and stable society; to understand factors that may influence extremist activities; to be astute in contemporary political affairs; to develop dispositions that will make more individuals more tolerant, or conversely, make individuals to be more vigilant against terrorism. An examination of various lesson plans will highlight the emphases offered that attend to each of these rationales.

We open up this critical debate to a broader political level in Chapter 3 in considering how such issues develop and evolve both at state and local policy. We consider the emphases and subtle omissions of how 9/11 and 7/7 have been constructed by the UK and the United States, and examine how that has significant implications for educators. This in turn leads to questions about the nature of knowledge itself. Questions arise such as: Is our 'knowledge' about terrorism and extremism simply the construction of those in power in the West, designed to fill the vacuum created by the collapse of communism? Are the constructions of knowledge of communities outside the West equally valid? How do we know? These questions raise concerns about the kinds of values we can legitimately promote with the school, and what values schools should be neutral about.

Chapter 4 attends to the pedagogical aspects of teaching controversial issues in the classroom, particularly related to teacher facilitation and teacher neutrality. How should terrorism and extremism be addressed in schools? Should controversial issues be facilitated by the teacher to allow for open dialogue? To what extent should teachers remain neutral on the issue? Is there a moral duty of educators to persuade students to behave in a certain way? Does providing a certain perspective lead to charges of indoctrination? Within these moral dilemmas, this chapter has two overarching aims: the first would be to offer ways in which teachers might broach the topic in highlighting the moral and practical implications of addressing such controversial topics in the classroom; the second would be to highlight the link between the issue of terrorism and extremism to that of political and moral education.

We come full circle in our deliberations of this debate in the final chapter, and consider whether educators can consider some principles in which to guide their actions on how to address terrorism and extremism in schools. In drawing the aims of the previous chapters together, Chapter 5 provides some normative recommendations to guide educators and policymakers in the task of discerning whether the issue of extremism and terrorism are a necessary component of developing politically active and engaged individuals in contemporary civil society. I conclude the following: that the issue of terrorism and extremism is a necessary and fundamental component that should be addressed in the curriculum; events such as 9/11 and 7/7 must be situated within the broader historical and political backdrop that give rise to such events, along with examining current inequitable circumstances that ostracize and marginalize certain groups to consider more extremist actions; and open facilitation and neutrality is an insufficient stance for teachers and schools to take, and must be situated within a larger moral framework.

CHAPTER ONE

The 'War on Terror' – Terrorism, Extremism and the Classroom

Terrorism and extremism are not new phenomena – far from it in fact. Terrorism and extremism have been effective and widely used techniques throughout history (Laqueur, 1977). They have not been relegated to one religion, but have spanned a number of religious and political groups – from Judaism, Islam, Hinduism, Christianity and atheism, to the political uprisings in the French Revolution, Marx and Bukinin, Irish nationalists and Russian anarchists to name but a few (Richardson, 2007, p. 23). While the ways in which terrorism have been brought on are significantly different in their tactics and devices to instil fear among a citizenry, the impact to instil fear has largely has had similar consequences. Law (2009) writes:

Clodius Pulcher, the Roman patrician, who used murderous gangs to intimidate his opponents; the dagger-wielding sacarii of Judea who hoped to provoke a war with the Romans; twelfth-century assassins who killed and terrorized their Muslim rivals; medieval scholars who quoted scripture to justify killing rulers – all these are examples of terrorism, and all predate the word 'terrorism' in revolutionary France.

(2009, p. 1)

Yet, the visual impact of the World Trade Center towers falling to the ground on real-time television, together with the current rise and fear of Islamic terrorism, created a wave of media frenzy and panic among the public citizenry in much of the Western industrialized nations. And while a palpable fear and anxiety of 9/11 created interest and sympathy from around the world, many non-English countries found the event troubling but not necessarily unsurprising nor creating undue anxiety and panic among the general public. A notable response from individuals (particularly in non-Western developing nations) noted that the atrocities of a few thousand people being killed paled in comparison to the widespread famine, poverty and long-standing civil wars and uprisings in many of their own countries. The panic and anxiety was again to be relived on 7 July 2005 when Islamic terrorists attacked the public transport systems in London.

Following the events of 9/11, various groups grappled with how to deal with the event and to address the initial grief and shock, the ensuing anger, and how to appropriately remember and honour those individuals. For schools, external pressure and internal debates became apparent. Government policies were developed and implemented that would have direct and indirect implications for schools and teachers.[3] Schools would now have to grapple with how to address students' concerns, fears and discussions that surrounded the terrorist activity. This would later be followed by wide-ranging and heated debates about the ways in which terrorism and extremism might be addressed in the curriculum.

---

[3] I will allude to these government policies in further detail in the coming chapters.

Pause for thought

To start us off, let us create a moment of reflection and consider your starting assumptions.

- How did you react to the events of 9/11 and 7/7?
- In what ways did you find yourself directly or indirectly implicated?
- If you were a teacher or a professor, did you have to adapt your lesson plans to address the events?
- In what ways did the media address the events?

To elucidate this debate, let us now turn to the United States and the United Kingdom to see the ways in which extremism and terrorism became more apparent in schools following the attacks.

The United States

It is clear and almost trite to state that 9/11 had an enormous impact on the American nation. The initial concern of schools immediately following the event was to address the fear, grief and anxiety of children. Those schools in Manhattan nearest to the 9/11 attacks note the early days following the attacks, not having a manual, crisis plan or emergency strategy that could prepare them for this. Many schools would start with the simple question: 'Does anyone want to say something about what happened?' (Lent, 2006, p. 7). Through drawings, poems and discussions, teachers and students attempted to work through how to make sense of the event. As one principal noted, 'By the way, this is not in the principal's manual' (Dolch, 2002, p. 31). Principals and teachers had not only to make sense of the event for themselves personally, but would now have to attend to the needs of their students.

Numerous counselling policies and procedures were put in place to address their sense of security and the general well-being of children. A number of studies indicated that the percentage of students who had significant anxiety and stress was notable. 'About 8 percent of the 4th through 12th graders surveyed were deemed to have suffered "major depression," 10 percent showed signs of "generalized anxiety," and 16 percent had agoraphobia—the fear of being in public places. More than 10 percent reported several symptoms consistent with post-traumatic stress disorder. The numbers were higher for youngsters who attended schools near the site of the World Trade Center' (Hoff, 2002, p. 3). Unsurprisingly, the focus in schools in the first year following 9/11 entailed putting into place a number of counselling strategies for students to cope and address the emotional stress that was put on them.

A number of children's books dealing with 9/11 followed soon thereafter. Books targeted to younger readers (aged 4 and above), tended to focus on narratives of heroism, personal anecdotal stories of triumph and courage, with illustrated pictorial images rather than actual footage of the day. *Fireboat* (Kalman, 2005) and *September Roses* (Winter, 2004) attempt to sooth children's anxieties and emphasize the positive aspects rather than the political complexity and tragedy itself (cited in Brocklehurst, 2011). Often referred to as 'bibliotherapy' or 'trauma' literature, others have questioned whether such depictions provide closure or reassurance for children who have access to the more political contentious and vivid accounts of 9/11 (Connelly, 2008; Brocklehurst, 2011). We will return to this question later in the book, but for now, let us move on and consider the multiple ways in which 9/11 was taken up in the United States.

In light of September 11, debates about how this event should be included in the civics curricula became prominent, not only among educators, but also from various external prominent members of the American public and external non-profit and lobby organizations. External organizations took the lead in attempting to address September 11 in meaningful ways in schools. *Rethinking Schools*, a progressive non-profit organization based in Milwaukee, Wisconsin, quickly published a collection of scholarly essays from various contributors on ways in which to teach about and discuss 9/11. The foreword of the special issue is telling, and provides a glimpse into the way this organization thought that schools should contend with the broader issues including and beyond 9/11:

> As educators committed to social justice, we believe that students need something different than a daily recitation of the Pledge of Allegiance. Whether we teach elementary students or older

ones, young people need global education. All students, starting with the youngest, need to develop empathy for people who are different or live under different conditions. They need to learn basic geography and history, and they must unlearn damaging stereotypes. And we can help students develop other critical skills: to question the policies of our government, to consider alternatives, to ask about who benefits and who suffers from particular policy choices, to evaluate media coverage of world events. We need to direct students' attention to the broad trends that continue to make the world an unequal and dangerous place.

(Kohn, 2001, p. 1)

Going beyond the patriotic images of America is what is required, rather than simply flag-waving, patriotic Americans. Kohn suggests that the way to measure how well students can understand the complex issues that surround not only the events leading up to 9/11 but also the longer precursors of inequality and injustice is to consider 'the extent to which the next generation comes to under-stand – and fully embrace – this simple truth: The life of someone who lives in Kabul or Baghdad is worth no less than the life of someone in New York or from our neighborhood' (ibid., p. 5).

A much different stance was taken by the Thomas Fordham Foundation. The tone is set in the introductory piece by Chester Finn Jr, which provides unwavering support for the actions taken by the then administration. 'Hurrah for President Bush and his stalwart team for instantly recognizing both the act of war that was visited upon us that bright September morning and the nature of our foe' (Finn, 2002, p. 4). In critiquing some of the pedagogical advice given to responding to September 11 (like that of *Rethinking Schools*), the collection of articles suggest that educators ought to resist the left-leaning advice given that advocates for the promotion of 'multiculturalism, feelings, relativism and tolerance but short on history, civics and patriotism' (ibid., p. 5). In its stead, the collection emphasizes themes of patriotism, freedom and democracy. Agresto (2002), for instance, suggests that if we are to teach about diversity, we should teach about how different Western and Islam perspectives are, rather than attempting to suggest that everyone has common values toward peace and tolerance. In this way, Agresto makes a parallel between Islam and Hitler, where few individuals would attempt to suggest that Hitler was a good individual and instead individuals should 'rightly hate him' (*ibid.*, p. 12). Comparisons are to be sought and distinctions are to be made under this perspective that labels right from wrong, good from evil, decency from immorality.

From a militaristic perspective, Lieutenant Colonel Jeffrey Adams (a retired US Army man), along with Joshua Sinai, a senior analyst on terrorism issues at Analytic Services (ANSER) devised a concise booklet on combating terrorism in schools and universities. *Protecting Schools and Universities from Terrorism: A Guide for Administrators and Teachers* (2003) does not provide lesson plans or curricular ideas on terrorism, but instead draws attention to raising awareness on potential forms of terrorism that may occur in the school. It is written with the assumption that schools and universities are potential sites of terrorist activity. The authors start with the premise that terrorists' intentions are to incite fear and anxiety across society, and given this, schools and universities provide random and unpredictable sites that particularly target vulnerable individuals thus undermining the general citizenry's confidence and stability (*ibid.*, p. 3). To combat this threat, schools are asked to take a proactive stance against the possible threat of terrorism in schools. In addressing the needs of students and teachers, the booklet recommends having counselling resources available to deal with the psychological and emotional needs following a terrorist attack, and to meet collectively to discuss the fears and anxieties in building a strong collective network. One of the recommendations made to reassure the student body is for principals and staff to watch for signs of distressed individuals and those particularly who are 'quiet', 'distracted' or with general changes to their normal behaviour. It also suggests that leaders of the institution should 'spend time walking through the school building and visiting classrooms. This leadership activity strongly reduces anxiety in both teachers and students' (*ibid.*, 16). Following these tips, the book then turns to the potential ways in which schools and universities may be attacked and how to protect against it, including conventional terrorism (e.g. bombs and explosive devices), chemical terrorism (e.g. how chemical agents may affect water, air or ventilation systems, or if they explode nearby), biological terrorism (e.g. the ways in which to spread bacteria and viruses such as smallpox, anthrax or botulism), and nuclear and radiological terrorism. The booklet concludes with a template for developing a disaster planning action to put into effect should such an attack occur.

Although presumably the intent of the booklet is to provide

concise information about potential threats to one's institution and
how to take certain precautions, the unintentional repercussion
is that it becomes alarmist in its very nature of the numerous
and drastic ways in which schools may be compromised sites
of terrorist activity. And if the sole intention is to identify an
emergency school plan to be proactive and prevent future possible
attacks, then it may prove a valuable resource. Yet, it goes beyond
this very mandate, and suggests ways in which the booklet can
teach terrorism. It makes three recommendations:

- Remind students of the value of living in a country
  that respects individual liberty, freedom of expression
  and religious belief, and the rule of law. Talk about the
  principles that led to the independence of our country and
  why these principles are still important today.

AND

- Encourage your students to participate in constructive
  activities related to the ongoing war on terrorism.

AND

- Many images on television of terrorist incidents or war
  are frightening, even to adults. Reduce or eliminate the
  presence of television news programs in the classrooms.

(*ibid.*, p. 17)

The advice offered here in addressing terrorism to students remains
ambiguous, undefined and potentially conflicting. The first recommendation takes a patriotic stance from a historical and contemporary
perspective, without necessarily addressing either how these values
apply to substantive issues or when competing values exist among
its citizenry. Discussed in a vacuous way, the recommendation
becomes a narrow rhetorical device to rally American citizens. The
second recommendation does little to guide the teacher who may be
grappling with how to address terrorism in the classroom. Again,
however, the emphasis on developing constructive activities lies in
focusing on the 'ongoing war on terrorism'. The perception is that
as a class (and nation) the activities are to combat terrorism, rather
than understanding the complex factors that underpin terrorism and
extremist activities. And the final recommendation suggests a reluctance to engage with news programmes. While the graphic media

portrayal of terrorist events are evident and need to be tempered with age-appropriateness, it seems misguided to ignore the fact that many children would have been privy to such images, and will need to discuss these issues. The third recommendation lacks a nuance that needs to balance a child's exposure to events with how to address and acknowledge that the events have occurred rather than ignore it given its difficult subject nature.

The ways in which terrorism and extremism are addressed differ drastically. In the early grades, a prevalence of developing the patriotic values of freedom of association, religion and speech are emphasized based around American independence and the founding constitution. The Public Broadcasting Service (PBS) website, 'America Responds', dedicates a webpage with links of suggested lesson plans to address the events of September 11. In the early grades, more focus is given to understanding one's heritage and values and typically highlighting similarities and differences between other groups within America, culminating in developing an American flag for the classroom. Another lesson plan targeted from pre-K to fifth grade suggests teaching about the symbolism and history behind the American flag with supplementary craft ideas for children. Middle-school children's lesson plans might entail a more historical analysis, which is then to be applied to contemporary pressing events. One lesson plan suggests teaching times of conflict such as the treatment of American citizens of Japanese and German descent, and the interconnected theme of assigning blame to a particular group of individuals or nations. This is to be contrasted with contemporary examples found in the form of 'ethnic conflict, discrimination, and stereotyping at home and abroad' (PBS website, 2010). Another lesson plan recommends that middle-school children consider the ways in which countries and organizations respond to emergency events, both natural and man-made.

High-school lesson plans offered on the PBS website suggest more debate and discussion surrounding terrorism. The 'Taming Terrorism' lesson plan aims to increase students' awareness in strategies to eradicate terrorism. Starting from their personal experience and the premise that the September 11 attacks were 'among the most terrible attacks in the world in terms of loss of life and the nature of the terrorists' crimes' (*ibid.*), students are asked to recall their knowledge of the attacks of September 11, 2001. Following this, they are to then asked to contrast this with other terrorist attacks both locally and abroad. The third task asks students to identify characteristics found in terrorists, and offers the 'Hunting Bin Laden' site as a useful resource. The final two tasks culminate in locating external organizations found in the UN and Homeland Security to see the ways in which they attempt to reduce terrorism, and suggest ways that students might strategize about reducing terrorist activities. In asking students to compare the various policies and tactics by various organizations the aim is that students will be better able to analyse and critique the policies used to combat terrorism.

The final lesson plan on the PBS website suggests that classrooms have a map of the world in order that high-school students can identify various geographical areas that are of particular relevance to American foreign policy. In highlighting countries such as Afghanistan, the aim of this lesson plan is to look at the historical, political and religious battles between the United States and foreign countries and evaluate their effectiveness in conflict resolution. According to the lesson plan, the ease of this topic can be readily made available by utilizing: World, US and Afghanistan maps; historical information; paper, pen, art supplies; and developing a Venn diagram or chart.

Despite the overwhelming amount of resources emanating from various political spectrums, lobby groups and external media and non-profit organizations, school textbooks seem on the periphery of developing substantive lesson plans around September 11. Most high schools acknowledge the event, and provide a historical and narrative account. Yet even the most basic of facts are often missing from textbooks. Now over a decade since the attacks of 9/11, it fails to take into the consideration that many of the students now entering secondary schools would have no recollection of the day's events. The omission of this basic information in textbooks assumes that children have a basic knowledge of the events that occurred leading up to, during and following the events of September 11. It further valorizes the tragedy and the perception that this particular terrorist event was one of the most significant events of the world in the past century. It is quick to move on to the heroic efforts of the public services, and the mourning of the citizenry thereafter. What it emphasizes in the narrative, emotional aspects of the event, it is scant on the substantive issues leading up to, and following the event. The lessons plans offer little advice to foster critical debate and analysis of terrorism and extremism in any meaningful context. Bill Bigelow and Bob Peterson (2005) critique this approach:

> The challenge for educators is not merely to describe these dangers, but to offer students the tools to help them explain today's world — to help them acquire a critical global literacy. Because only explanation offers the hope of addressing root causes of social problems.
>
> (2005, p. 26)

This has been reiterated at numerous levels whereby what is included in the textbooks is largely influenced by those states that have larger student populations (and thus larger purchasing and lobbying power). This is particularly relevant for those topics that are considered sensitive, controversial and may be perceived as 'unpatriotic' (see, for example: Evans, 2004; Loewen, 2009; Leahey, 2009).

The development of curricular material has been a matter of much debate. For instance, much public attention was drawn to the Texas school board that made a number of revisions and amendments to textbooks in the areas of history, economics and sociology (McKinnley Jr, 2010). Texas happens to be the largest buyer of textbooks in the United States, and thus has considerable influence in deciding curricular emphasis in the textbooks. Corporations and private companies often fund and sponsor textbooks for distribution in schools (Leahey, 2010, pp. 29–33). The judgements and decisions that are ultimately made will influence and direct the nature of the curriculum including: How and which authors are chosen to write the manuscript? How are themes and topics introduced, presented and emphasized (or neglected)? When are second and revised editions tweaked and edited or, conversely, substantively rewritten given a major change of events? Given the diverse and contested way in which terrorism and extremism is addressed in the larger public debate, it should be of little surprise that conflicting messages and emphases are provided in the curricular textbooks. The problem of curriculum development in textbooks is not limited to the issue of the inclusion (or exclusion) of terrorism and extremism in civics curriculum, but extends to a much larger debate beyond the scope of this book. Yet, in considering the specific issue of whether terrorism should be taught in schools, one must nonetheless understand the circumstances that shape and inform the debate.

Pause for thought

In the previous section, I alluded to a number of ways in which the events of 9/11 are being addressed in schools. At this point, take a moment to consider to what extent you would feel comfortable in addressing the events of 9/11 from the following perspectives:

The teacher
- To what extent should a teacher address 9/11 in the classroom?
- Does it matter whether you teach elementary or secondary levels?
- What emphasis should be taught in relaying the events? Historical, political, psychological, sociological?
- Should teachers bear the burden in teaching these events?
- Should this be better handled in the private discussions of the home?
- Should the topic of terrorism be focused on 9/11 or should it involve a broader discussion around the notion of terrorism in other contexts?

The student
- How would you like to be informed of the events of 9/11? By your parents, community or schools?
- Should the teaching of 9/11 be part of the formal curriculum? Should a day of remembrance be created in honouring the victims of 9/11?
- Would you feel comfortable in discussing the issue with your classmates or teacher?

The parent
- To what extent should schools teach about 9/11 or acts of terrorism?
- To what extent do you think this discussion is a private or public discussion?
- What emphasis should be given in teaching 9/11? Should the focus be on acts of heroism, grief, courage, rebuilding a nation, patriotism, security, forgiveness, toleration?

The ways in which American educators have addressed the events of 9/11 are as wide and divergent as the nation itself. For the most part, educators are left to deal with how they discuss this with students both in the short and long term. Despite the wide variance in what should be taught, teachers have been reprimanded (and at times, dismissed) by school boards, parents and communities for not teaching it in a way that they felt was inappropriate. I will talk more about this in Chapter 2.

The United Kingdom's response

Soon after the 7/7 attacks on London's public transport systems, early attempts to address terrorism in schools largely came in the form of identifying potential extremists targeted by the central government, and attempts at addressing the issue in schools at a curricular level. The educational press carried many headlines of the following kind:

- **'First rumblings of a call to arms.** How did we arrive at global jihad? A student researching the madrassas of Northern Pakistan stumbled across some answers' (*Times Educational Supplement*, 21 July 2006).

- **'Classes to stop suicide bombs?** Citizenship as a subject is still finding its feet, but supporters have high hopes for it, reports Michael Shaw' (*Times Educational Supplement*, 23 June 2006).

- **'Fighting the war on dogma.** Universities combat extremism by exposing untruth and teaching critical thinking, argues Bhiku Parekh' (*Times Higher*, 28 July 2006).

- **'Staff must "identify" extremism.** State guidance asks academics to monitor student activity and "ask for help"' (*Times Educational Supplement*, 20 October 2006).

- **'Terrorist packs withdrawn.** Teaching packs based on the September 11 atrocities, which invited pupils to imagine organising a terrorist attack, have been withdrawn from schools' (*Times Educational Supplement*, 22 September 2006).

- 'The spy who taught me. Draft plans to monitor "Asian-looking" students spark fears that Muslims aren't welcome on campus' (*The Guardian*, 24 October 2006).

- 'As a student, I was in the front line ... Shiraz Maher, a former member of the radical group Hizb ut-Tahir, says universities have been wilfully blind to extremist groups recruiting on campus' (*Times Higher*, 27 October 2006).

The emphasis in schools and higher educational institutions was largely focused on vigilance of instructors to alert the authorities should they suspect peculiar or suspicious activity that might warrant further security measures.

At the central government level, policy frameworks were being devised and implemented throughout the United Kingdom. Most notably, *Preventing Violent Extremism Agenda: A strategy for delivery* henceforth referred to as the PVE agenda (2008) was published and distributed largely in direct response to the 7/7 Islamic terrorist events in London. Despite its acknowledgement that terrorism has been prevalent in the UK prior to the 2007 London bombings (most notably throughout the twentieth century by the IRA), its mandate is specific in combating the increased fear of Islamic attacks against the UK. The introduction is forthright in their target against Islamic extremists. It states:

> The most severe terrorist threat currently comes from individuals and groups who distort Islam to attempt to justify murder and their attacks on our shared values. There are other extremists trying to sow division in this country, against whom the Government is also taking action, for example by tackling the hateful views and actions of extreme right-wing groups. But the most severe threat comes from those who hijack the peaceful religion of Islam as a basis for their attacks. The Prevent strategy sets out how we are addressing this threat to improve the security of the UK in the long term.
>
> (DCSFa, 2008, p. 5)

Despite the United Kingdom's long history of terrorism, the *Preventing Violent Extremism* agenda is more troubling in its direct labelling of a religious group – that of Islam. Although the government attempts to be subtle regarding the generalization about Islam as a group and fundamentalists within the Islamic groups, the potential repercussions for Muslim groups in the UK seem formidable in being accepted and integrated within the 'mainstream' British culture. Islam becomes the villain with the state having the upper hand in putting pressure on groups they deem to be a threat. I will discuss this further in Chapter 2, but for now let us move on to the education directives from the PVE agenda.

A teaching and learning supplemental toolkit is handily provided to schools to help implement the *Preventing Violent Extremism* agenda (DCSFb, 2008). Continuing on the increased fear of rising Islamic extremism in the UK, the *Learning Together to be Safe: A toolkit to help schools contribute to the prevention of violent extremism* toolkit focuses on combating the potential developments of extremist activities in mosques, schools and universities. The toolkit provides a four-pronged approach to addressing extremism. The strategy aims to:

- raise awareness among schools of the threat from violent extremist groups and the risks for young people

- provide information about what can cause violent extremism, about preventative actions taking place locally and nationally and about where schools can get additional information and advice

- help schools understand the positive contribution they can make to empowering young people to create communities that are more resilient to extremism, and protecting the well-being of particular pupils or groups who may be vulnerable to being drawn into violent extremist activity

- provide advice on managing risks and responding to incidents.

(DCSFb, 2008, p. 5)

The rationale suggests that by implementing this four-pronged approach, schools will reduce the increased prevalence of grooming extremist behaviours and thoughts among considered at-risks groups. In addition to reducing extremist behaviours through activities, it is clear that one of the key roles of this agenda is for schools to be a watchdog for identifying potential extremist individuals in their classes. The first primary aim recommends raising awareness among schools. The emphasis in the booklet suggests becoming attentive to individuals who may take on the characteristics found in extremists, such as a perception that their family or community has been unduly disadvantaged, and that the state does not attempt to resolve such underpinning injustices that they perceive to be occurring. Following these assumptions, extremists are said to justify violent means in which to change the present circumstances. Using single narratives, extremists attempt to recruit at-risk individuals by providing a narrow (perhaps distorted) interpretation of the historical, political and ideological circumstances that disenfranchise that individual and their group. Again, the toolkit provides key bullets for consideration in attempting to identity potential extremists that may be involved in violent extremism. The individual:

- may begin with a search for answers to questions about identity, faith and belonging

- may be driven by the desire for 'adventure' and excitement

- may be driven by a desire to enhance the self-esteem of the individual and promote their 'street cred'

- is likely to involve identification with a charismatic individual and attraction to a group which can offer identity, social network and support.

(*ibid.*, p. 17)

It becomes apparent that the overwhelming objective is for schools to identify potential threats, and if need be, become an informant for the police in identifying potential extremists.

Given its specific attention for applying the *Preventing Violent Extremism* agenda in schools, it would be remiss that the toolkit did not provide assistance in *how* schools should attend to this issue. The second objectives sets out the following aims: to provide principles in which to adapt the curriculum to address violent extremism and human rights in the curriculum; highlight teaching and learning strategies to raise controversial issues in the classroom, and; suggest ways in which external organizations may provide support. While the section highlights the areas of the curriculum where violent extremism may be addressed, it does little to provide substantive recommendations in how that might be achieved. The rhetoric of fostering critical debate, providing safe spaces in which to debate and valuing diversity and freedom of expression is liberally used throughout the section. Beyond these phrases, it suggests that schools review and develop the curriculum to address violent extremism in their particular local contexts. While the recommendations are purposely intended not to be prescriptive or exhaustive, the burden rests with schools in articulating a cohesive curriculum that attends to both the sensitive and controversial nature of extremism and terrorism. And if the threat of violent extremism is on the rise, as the booklet suggests, then the significance of schools to address this issue in meaningful ways that will not only reduce extremist behaviour but develop better respect and social cohesion is a tall order for educators to fill. Once again schools are burdened with fixing the ills of society.

Conversely, in response to the *Preventing Violent Extremism* agenda and the *Learning Together to be Safe* toolkit, the Muslim Council of Britain also responded by publishing *Towards Greater Understanding: Meeting the needs of Muslim pupils in state schools: Information & Guidance for Schools* (2007). The foreword by the Muslim Council of Britain is clear in its objectives: to highlight the significant proportion of Muslims living in Britain, comprising of the largest religious minority; to note the overwhelming percentage (96 per cent) of Muslim children who attend mainstream state education; and the need for better understanding and inclusion of Muslims within the pluralist English society. The report attempts to redress the inaccurate perceptions of Muslims portrayed in the media. It states:

> The current climate, in which there is much negative portrayal of Islam and Muslim requires that this be given greater priority and impetus to ensure that Muslim pupils are appropriately accommodated for and become an integral part of mainstream school life and thereby of society as a whole.
>
> (2007, p. 7)

This foreword seeks a different approach; schools should foster an inclusive ethos that develops good practices that are welcoming and respectful of faith identity and religious needs. Further, the report is a response to the anti-Islamic portrayal found in official government documents, and provides normative recommendations about how to create cohesion in a diverse student population.

Whereas the emphasis for the *Learning Together to be Safe* toolkit attends to potential risks of extremism forming in schools, this report attends to some of the obstacles that Muslim pupils face commonly in state schools in feeling isolated or marginalized. Different aspects of dress codes for Muslim children are highlighted in the document, requesting that schools accommodate for dress within their uniform policies. I have written extensively on defining the parameters of religious and cultural dress in schools elsewhere (Gereluk, 2008), and have argued that a rigid stance on dress codes and uniform policies both creates further divisions for those unable to express their religion through dress, and for those pupils who are not exposed to issues of diversity in real and tangible ways (Gereluk, 2009). It is unsurprising that the Muslim Council of Britain has noted this obstacle that further exacerbates the tensions and backlash between Muslim and non-Muslim children who are restricted to attend certain schools that will allow for religious accommodation in their uniform policies.

Another notable obstacle that Muslim children face is that little accommodation is commonly made to provide halal meals within the school, particularly where there are greater numbers of Muslim children enrolled in a particular school. Not clearly marking halal or vegetarian meals for school lunches or activities may cause unnecessary conflict. Observance of prayer notes that only two prayers are required during the school day: one at midday and one between mid-afternoon and sunset should the pupil remain at the school longer. Religious festivals such as Eid and Ramadan should be noted and acknowledged by the school. Finally, curricular issues that may conflict with the Islamic faith are highlighted and asked that accommodation be made, particularly relating to physical education, sex and relationship education, music or drama. Of the above listed recommendations in the document, the last one is arguably most contentious. Much debate surrounds the extent to which religious and cultural accommodation should be given for parents to raise their children within their particular belief system that may conflict with the aims stated in various public education systems (Bridges, 1984; McLaughlin, 1984, Halstead, 1994, 1997; Reich, 2002; Merry, 2007; Gereluk, 2010; Corngold, 2011). A delicate balance then exists between the religious accommodations of parents and their communities with the state's obligation to protect the future interests of children. Michael Merry states, 'Considering the challenges that

Muslims in particular face in the post 9/11world, Islamic schools carry special significance for how Muslims living in the West wish to carve out identities for themselves and their children that are true not only to their individual or collective faith(s), but also to the societies of which they are an integral part' (2007, p. x). While this is a contested matter regarding parental exemptions of certain curricular subjects for their children, the general tone of the report is that Muslims are a prevalent demographic in Britain and schools ought to aim for inclusive practices that welcome (rather than ostracize) Muslims within their schools.

Pause for thought

An interesting tension exists between the *Preventing Violent Extremism* and *Learning Together to be Safe* documents published by the British government and that of the *Meeting the needs of Muslim pupils in state schools* document published by the Muslim Council of England.

The documents have very different mandates and objectives. Consider:

- To what extent should schools (and teachers) be attentive to suspicious or high-risk activities in their pupils?
- To what extent should schools accommodate for religious or cultural beliefs? Are there parameters in making certain accommodations? Where should schools draw the line and what criteria should be used in making such distinctions?
- Is it possible for schools to create inclusive environments without addressing the inequalities or forms of discriminations that occur at a broader societal level? Why or why not?

Conflicting values in England: the move towards Britishness

The events of 7/7 did little to alleviate the concerns that multiculturalism had failed in the eyes of many in Britain (Gereluk and Race, 2007b). This would be further exacerbated by a large civil disturbance that occurred between Afro-Caribbean and Asian youths on the streets of Lozells Road, Birmingham on 22 October 2005. During the disturbances, shops were attacked – many of them owned by Pakistanis – cars were set alight and riot police were bombarded by bricks and glass. Four people were stabbed, which led to one death, and 80 offences were committed during the course of the evening. The attacks were largely predicated on a rape allegation made by a teenage Afro-Caribbean girl who stated that she had been attacked by a group of Pakistani boys earlier in the week. The allegation was leaked to a pirate radio station which exacerbated the situation and created further increased racial tensions: tensions that were already fragile and precarious between the two minority groups.[4]

Social problems and divisions, underlined by the Birmingham riots in October 2005 highlighting social problems and divisions between Asian and Afro-Caribbean communities, are not new. Social issues – namely poverty, unemployment and exclusion – were noted by Rex and Moore (1969) in Birmingham over 30 years ago. Their social research highlighted that parents and children from Indian and Pakistani communities chose not to accept schools' teaching patterns and value systems. The communities' resistance was visible in their processes of non-socialization in terms of attitudes and behaviour patterns both in schools and local communities. Both parents and children refused to change their value systems, thereby refusing to totally integrate into the majority community.

The fears that extremist groups were on the rise in England with the terrorists being born in England, along with the civil riots in autumn 2005, helped to gain public sympathy for a call to relinquish the ideals of multiculturalism towards a notion of 'Britishness'. Developing a sense of Britishness was on the rise along with the assimilationist policies to reflect this new public ideal. The Commission for Equality and Human Rights, formerly the Commission of Racial Equality in England, aims to strengthen race relations among communities. This has included creating better lines of communication between voluntary groups, and similarly minimizing rumours that might exacerbate potentially volatile

---

[4]The description of the 2005 civil riots was published earlier in Gereluk, D. and Race, R. (2007) 'Multicultural Tensions in England, France and Canada: Contrasting approaches and consequences', *International Studies in Sociology of Education*, 17 (1 and 2), pp. 113–29.

racial problems. Yet in a 2005 speech, 'After 7/7: sleepwalking to segregation', Trevor Phillips, then head of the Commission for Racial Equality, suggested that the ideals of multiculturalism had led to more animosity and segregation among ethnic groups rather than social cohesion. He argued that:

> In recent years we've focused far too much on the 'multi' and not enough on the common culture. We've emphasized what divides us over what unites us ... This is not only, or even principally, about Muslims. But the aftermath of 7/7 forces us to assess where we are. And here is where I think we are: we are sleepwalking our way to segregation.
>
> (Phillips, 2005, p. 5)

These remarks resonate with an earlier speech that Phillips gave in 2004, where he suggested that perhaps multiculturalism was of another era and should be scrapped (Phillips, 2004). Without taking Phillips out of context, his statements suggest that the pendulum has swung away from multiculturalism, and they are more suggestive of developing more central integrationist, common values alongside the value of diversity in Britain. Otherwise, he warns that multiculturalism that favours only diversity without shared values threatens to create a more segregated, isolated society. Phillips' controversial statements continue to receive fierce criticism and opposition and are indicative of the attempt to balance a very pluralist British society within integrationist social policies. Similar sentiments are on the rise throughout continental Europe, most notably in the Netherlands, Germany and France.

Since the 2005 bombings in London, developing a sense of Britishness has taken on a more prominent stage in the political debates and has received cross-party support (Brown, 2000; Cameron, 2007). Multiculturalism has lost its appeal, with the focus on diversity leading to increased alienation and segregation. The view toward Britishness is seen as moving towards common values and British achievements toward a view to 'restore community cohesion and a sense of civic belonging' (Johnson, 2007). The underpinning assumption in putting forth an agenda of Britishness is that allowing for a conflict of values will inevitably lead to a weaker civil society; conversely, shared common values will lead to consensus and a sense of harmony among the polis (Edyvane, 2011,

p. 76). A national identity is sought – one that puts forth the ideal of 'one nation, one community' (Blair, 2003). Similar sentiments were expressed by Gordon Brown, who noted that there was a need to stop the 'Balkanization of Britain' through its mislaid policies of multiculturalism in combination with increased immigration and nationalist separatism (Brown, 2007). A growing sense of segregation among Britons both geographically and ideologically has called forth a resurgence towards a national identity.

The move towards integration has been echoed by Lord Ahmed who thought that the accommodations to minority racial groups had regressed the movement towards integration of immigrants to mainstream British society. Regarding the hijab worn by increasing numbers of women in Britain, Lord Ahmed thought that:

> The 'veil' is now a mark of separation, segregation and defiance against mainstream British culture ... There is nothing in the Koran to say that the wearing of a niqab is desirable, let alone compulsory. It's purely cultural ... They are a physical barrier to integration ... We need to re-engage as responsible British citizens and be seen once more as contributors to society rather than people who are a burden, living parallel lives.
>
> (cited in Herbert, 2007)

Clear identifying signifiers that create divisions are made in the comments by Lord Ahmed regarding the hijab and the niqab. Those who wear them should be regarded as being against the values of mainstream society – someone to be opposed, feared and assimilated. If they do not conform, they are a burden and a threat to the stability of Western civil society.

Haw (2009) notes the discontinuities in creating social cohesion among Muslim girls in a post-9/11 world and the tensions inherent between integration and separation among such diverse communities. And schools are stuck in the middle of such a debate:

> Schools and their local authorities are also called upon to mediate between a complex shift from accommodation of different ethnicities towards and accommodation of different and diverse individual identities as they struggle to maintain their own identity and academic reputation.
>
> (*ibid.*, p. 368)

The emerging and ongoing debates and policy directives all seem to indicate a closing in of accommodations to ethnic minorities in favour of a more secure social cohesion within mainstream British society.

The cry for social cohesion would again rear its head in the youth riots of summer 2011 where riots erupted throughout England from disenfranchised youths across the country. Businesses were looted, buildings set on fire, and new riots emerged with the use of instant messaging and social media devices to quickly mobilize other individuals. Over 1,800 arrests were made following the riots, and renewed debates about the need to fix a broken society were brought forth. Prime Minister David Cameron contended that the riots were a function of 'dysfunctional families' and simply a function of 'pure criminality' and a 'slow-motion moral collapse' that had failed in teaching their children about personal responsibility and developing a moral code (Sparrow, 2011).

Others critiqued Cameron's assessment of the cause of the riots. Although England has a long class-based history, a growing underclass was notable, with increasing numbers of individuals being entrenched in concentrated areas with few job prospects and overall declining economic fortunes. These long-term trends of poverty and disenfranchisement have 'obvious implications for the employment and educational opportunities of young people, as well as for how they perceive themselves and their future prospects' (White et al., 2011, p. 23).

Despite such indicators that suggest that the riots were more than 'pure criminality', there were calls for a renewed attention to fix the 'broken society'. Cameron stated:

> I can announce today that over the next few weeks, I and ministers from across the coalition government will review every aspect of our work to mend our broken society, on schools, welfare, families, parenting, addiction, communities, on the cultural, legal, bureaucratic problems in our society too; from the twisting and misrepresenting of human rights that has undermined personal responsibility, to the obsession with health and safety that has eroded people's willingness to act according to common sense – and consider whether our plans and programmes are big enough and bold enough to deliver the change that I feel this country now wants to see.
>
> (*ibid.*, p. 1)

Social cohesion would now come in the form of 'managing youth' through a multi-pronged process of being governed and watched to develop the moral dispositions that are found wanting by the prime minister. In this way, 'governments actively create and maintain standards of normative behaviour and dispositions ... Government policies in education and health determine what areas of young people's lives are emphasised and what are ignored' (Wyn, 2009, p. 57). The policies are overt in their intent to restore order and cohesion in a fractured society. The argument is that too much emphasis has been put forward toward personal rights to the exclusion of one's personal responsibilities, and a distortion occurs in how that plays out in today's youth. A new moral order is required to restore calm.

The events of 7/7, together with the growing sense of unease among the youth in the United Kingdom (most notably in the riots of 2005 and 2011) has called forth the need for more social cohesion and developing a sense of Britishness among its pupils. In putting forth this agenda, it does beg the question of what 'Britishness' entails given the diverse inhabitants in this country. Defining a certain identity based on Britishness does little to provide support to teachers who must teach this nebulous concept to their pupils. Breslin et al. (2006) reported their findings of citizenship education contending that the way in which Britishness was constructed in the classroom was generally equated to a notion of 'Englishness', also excluding other groups such as the Scottish, Welsh and Northern Irish. The overarching concern was that in developing a sense of Britishness might lead us down a slippery slope towards 'Indoctrination into a narrow, fixed, uncritical and intolerant nationalism' (*ibid.*, p. 21).

Maylor and Read's report (2006) on diversity and citizenship in the curriculum articulated similar concerns. Diversity issues often neglected the White Caucasians and the heterogeneity within this broad category. And when diversity was discussed, the focus largely attended to minority ethnic groups. Little discussion surrounded what it means to understand diversity within British society; instead focus was on attending to differences among ethnic groups without the broader contextual backdrop of how that would influence civil society (pp. 7–9). And further, the report noted that the way in which diversity might be taken up in a school was largely influenced by the extent of the diverse demographics of pupils. In those schools where there was a more homogenous 'White' demographic, issues of diversity were superficially addressed and thought of as unnecessary. In more multi-ethnic schools, diversity issues were more at the forefront of curriculum in acknowledging and understanding diversity within the specific contextual contexts.

The promotion of Britishness is clearly contested in how it positions individuals in the United Kingdom. Those living in England may regard Britishness as being equated to that of 'Englishness' and may feel further excluded or marginalized. Those individuals living in Scotland, Wales and Northern Ireland may not agree with the notion of a united national identity given a more contested history with the English and their sense of national supremacy over them (Andrews and Mycock, 2008). Proponents maintain that the promotion of 'Britishness' is an attempt to rekindle a sense of national identity built on the political and civic traditions that underpin the United Kingdom, most notably those of free speech, the rule of law, mutual tolerance and respect for equal rights (DfES, 2007). More cynically, some see Britishness as a political device 'designed to simultaneously placate the English middle classes and suppress the emergence of English nationalism' (Andrew and Mycock, p. 150).

Pause for thought

The move away from multiculturalism towards a notion of social cohesion and Britishness is gaining prominence and support. Such a view has direct implications for how we conceive and teach citizenship education.

On social cohesion:
- Should social cohesion be prioritized over that of multiculturalism?
- What does social cohesion entail?
- Is there a moral ethic that is required when we teach about social cohesion?

On Britishness:
- To what extent should schools teach Britishness?
- What values are inherent in the notion of Britishness?
- Can schools teach the values of both multiculturalism and Britishness? Are they complementary or competing values?

Conclusion

It is clear that a tension exists in a pluralist society. On the one hand, an underpinning principle in Western liberal democracies is that individuals can lead a life of their choosing that allows for the richness and celebration of diversity within the larger political sphere. That said, such freedom must also be tempered with a need to foster collective values in which to live cohesively. Although these two principles need not be mutually exclusive of each other, in times of increased uncertainty and anxiety about the safety and stability of a society (such as in the case of 9/11 and 7/7), the view of stability and security may outweigh the individual freedoms of liberty.

Now over a decade on from 9/11, little has been resolved in how we might address this in our schools and in our classes. Further, the conflicting documents offer little reassurance or consistency in how teachers might do so. In the coming chapters, we will grapple with how one might construct such a balance in schools and in the curriculum in attending to these difficult grey areas to reduce a potential conflict of 'us' and 'them' both within and beyond schools.

Further reading

In coming to understand how terrorism and extremism have been situated within particular government directives, it is recommended that you read the key government documents on this issue from the United Kingdom: *Preventing Violent Extremism* (DCSF, 2008), *Learning Together to be Safe* (DCSF, 2008), and the *Guidance on the Duty to Promote Community Cohesion* (DCSF, 2007).

You may also wish to consider some of the reports that have been published in response to these government documents. Of particular interest may be *Toward Greater Understanding* (Muslim Council of Britain, 2006), *Citizenship Education* (Breslin et al., 2006), and *Diversity and Citizenship in the Curriculum* (Maylor and Read, 2007).

The contrasting perspectives found in *Whose Wars: Teaching about the Iraq War and the War on Terrorism* (Rethinking Schools,

2005), and *September 11: What our children need to know* (Fordham Foundation, 2002), exemplifies the contested debate in America for how schools might address the events of 9/11.

Numerous psychological and counselling studies have been undertaken following September 11. For more in-depth discussion of this particular aspect of the 9/11 events, please see:

Lengua, L., Long, A., Smith, K. and Meltzoff, A. (2005) 'Pre-attack symptomatology and temperament as predictors of children's responses to the September 11 terrorist attacks', *Journal of Child Psychology and Psychiatry*, 46(6), 631–45.

Schuster, M. et al. (2001) 'A National Survey of Stress Reactions after the September 11, 2001, Terrorist Attacks', *The New England Journal of Medicine*, 345, 1507–12.

Stuber, J. et al. (2002) 'Determinants of Counseling for Children in Manhattan after the September 11 Attacks', *Psychiatric Services*, 53, 815–22.

CHAPTER TWO

To Broach or Not to Broach? That is the Question

Controversial topics such as terrorism are difficult to negotiate. It is unclear given the sensitivities of the topic whether it is best left in the hands of teachers, counsellors, or parents to broach the subject. We grapple with how much our children should watch breaking news clips about various attacks of terrorism and counter terrorism. On the one hand, we want our children to be informed; on the other hand, we are cautious about the unwanted anxiety and fear that this may cause (not to mention the way in which such events are portrayed in the media). Parents may not even have a sense to what extent children are exposed to such information, whether they see it on the internet, social networking sites, informal conversations in hallways and out of earshot of adults, or whether it is taught formally in the curriculum. And adults struggle about when such topics should be addressed. To what extent do we talk about these issues to young children, or keep them monitored and limited until they reach a level of maturity or age in which they can synthesize and work through these complexities. This is not an easy task, and one on which little consensus will be reached.

Given that we may never come to agreement, how are schools to address issues of terrorism and extremism? Should schools interrupt their daily lessons when events such as Osama Bin Laden being killed enter and cause a nation and the international world to take pause and comment? CNN was one of the leading news networks that used the death of Osama Bin Laden to create a debate about how one might address these issues with children. Yet, common to media, they used provocative statements to seduce their audience to tune in. In the opening tag lines prior to a debate on children and terrorism, Drew Plinsky (2011) offers up her services to show us the light: 'Now that Osama Bin Laden is dead, our kids are asking a lot of questions. How should you answer them? I'm here to help' (Plinsky, 2011). It is followed up with a more invasive tactic that is more personal and intimate in nature: 'Miss USA says she was groped during an airport pat-down. What is terrorism doing to us?' (*ibid.*, 2011).   These news stories raise the issues, but do so in a way that caters to parents' anxieties and concerns over the well-being of their children. Using both provocative and emotive techniques, the news programme provides little substantive advice for parents in addressing the issue. If parents feel inadequate in addressing the issue, commonly it is then left for schools to do so. If schools do address the issue, how are they to respond? Should teachers talk about the event in the larger political context of terrorism, or simply that this was a 'bad' man who was defeated? Should they talk about larger issues about patriotism, retribution or contemplation? Entering into such a debate, particularly in the public sphere such as a school, is a thorny and tricky endeavour. It is an incredibly difficult challenge for teachers who walk a tightrope, to raise awareness without offending or causing further animosity among students and their families in the student population in and beyond the school walls.

Pause for thought

Take a moment to think about where you stand on whether children should be informed about issues that arise from terrorist and extremist activities. As you reflect on the following, there is an implicit question about at what age you might consider it appropriate to teach children about such issues.

- Should children be exposed to watching and listening to media events as they unfold?
- Should an adult wait until the child asks a question about the event, or should the adult initiate such conversations?

Now that you have a rough idea of the ethical and moral dilemmas that are inherent in teaching this topic, let us take a step back and consider some of the reasons that one might broach the issue of terrorism and extremism in schools. A number of common justifications are used in addressing terrorism and extremism, including: to develop a more cohesive and stable society; to understand factors that may influence extremist activities; to be astute in contemporary political affairs; to develop dispositions that will make more individuals more tolerant, or conversely, make individuals more vigilant against terrorism. In the following sections, we will look at these reasons, and after each section consider some of the opportunities and challenges that each justification offers.

Justification one: to protect and create a stable society

When the general citizenry is at a heightened sense of anxiety and panic caused by terrorist attacks, a call for calm and stability often ensues. This was clearly the case for Americans who wanted reassurance and resilience which would manifest in various ways. Immediately following 9/11, Americans first wanted to feel comfort from their heightened levels of fear and anxiety. Those nearest to the attacks in New York City used a number of strategies in which to create a sense of routine and normalcy in the students' lives. Some teachers allowed parents to stay with their children in the classrooms for as long as the children or parents needed to stay. Others used strategies to empower students in letting them work through ideas of how they stayed safe during the bombings by drawing pictures and expressing their emotions. One young child drew a picture depicting two scenarios, one in which they were panicking with their parents, the other with them walking calmly, hand in hand. The child wrote, 'We didn't panik [sic] or get crazy. All we did was walk and ran and walk some more' (Lent, 2006, p. 9). The Christian Children's Fund (CCF), an organization that commonly provides funding and assistance to countries directly affected by war and poverty, helped to initiate a World Trade Center children's mural project, where children from all over the world could send their messages of hope, peace and solidarity to the children of New York City (Berberian, 2006, pp. 81–3). Another initiative, that of Project Renewal, was developed in 2002 to address the 'inner lives of students and educators' with activities designed to 'restore a positive sense of meaning and vitality to their lives and their careers' (Lantieri, 2006, pp. 114–15). Many students and educators expressed depression and fatigue at trying to make sense of the event and this project was aimed at trying to enable individuals to move forward in their lives.

Another clear attempt was to inculcate those values at the school level in a resurgence and resilience of national identity in the face of increased uncertainty and fear of the 'other': 'Group identification at the national level ... creates bonds of solidarity among all members, aligns individual interests with national welfare, and provides the motivation for being a good group member at the individual level ...' (Li and Brewer, 2004, p. 727). A run on American flags took place in stores across America, showing unwavering patriotic spirit in the face of tragedy. Renewed debates ensued about whether children should recite the Pledge of Allegiance in schools. There was a sense that Americans needed to take a unified stance that they would not succumb to the fear of terrorist actions.

While these patriotic symbolic gestures were both overt and explicit, other subtle government controls were put in place under the guise of taking a unified stance against terrorism. One of the justifications used for reducing one's civil liberties is that in trying to curtail further terrorist attacks a state may need to take invasive and swift arbitrary action that infringes on individual liberties. Tapping phones, looking at personal bank accounts, surveil-lance and search warrants without going through the necessary protocol are commonly justified as a necessary infringement of individual liberties in the larger threat against terrorism. Although the pressure to enact such measures may be external, such limitations are commonly self-inflicted by one's own state (Grayling, 2009, p. 2). The action is explicit and it is argued that uncertain times call for expedient action and order which outweigh the concerns for upholding the democratic principles that underpin Western societies. The list varies in terms of how security measures are put in place, but may include the power of the state to 'detain, inspect, question, collect personal information, intercept communications, and deploy new and more instruments of surveillance and monitoring' (*ibid.*, p. 15).

Coupled with restrictive civil liberties in the name of security, calls for a renewed patriotism and nationalism abound. Soon after the 9/11 attacks, President George Bush enacted The Patriot Act (2001) to increased military intervention in Afghanistan and Iraq abound. Both the political right and the political left used the 9/11 attacks to demonstrate who was more patriotic. George Bush used repeated phrases that enacted patriotic language to stir up a national sentimentalism in the 'War on Terror'. Given the patriotic fervour that occurred following 9/11, then presidential candidate, Senator Kerry, highlighted his role and involvement in the Vietnam War and the heroism that was bestowed (and challenged by the Swift Boat Veterans for Truth campaign). In the early days following 9/11, individuals had a sense of duty and urgency to do 'something' and display both their grief and solidarity as a nation. Symbolic gestures were visible with the raising of American flags in US homes. Some individuals felt an obligation and urgency to join the army as their patriotic duty, and at a farcical level terminology to show allegiance or resistance was notable with the changing of 'French fries' to 'Freedom fries' to show opposition to the French government's stance on Iraq. A veil of unity across political divisions is intended to create a sense of belonging and agreement. Yet, in doing so it creates two problems. First is that those who wish to challenge such unity may feel excluded, marginalized or targeted by the dominant discourse. Second, it lessens the ability to have a deliberative conversation about how best to move forward after such events. What is often required is a sense of unanimous consensus with little debate or discussion.

Rarely do schools position the debate about national stability and security in a liberal democratic society as the restriction of civil liberties as a positive value to espouse. Yet, such values may play out in the delivery of patriotism. Ben-Porath (2006) suggests that in times of long-term conflict or war, and acts of terrorism that threaten the stability of a nation, a narrowing of the citizenship curriculum may occur:

> Belligerent citizenship is distinctly characterized by a reinterpreted notion of key components of democratic citizenship, among them participation, unity and solidarity and public deliberation. In times of war these take the form of an emphasis on citizens' contribution to the country rather than on voluntary participation; support for social unity and patriotism over diversity; and consequently, the discouragement of open deliberation.
>
> (Ben-Porath, forthcoming)

Emphasis is concentrated on one's civic duty to one's nation, rather than on civic engagement and deliberation. And ironically, protecting one's individual freedom is used as a justification for allowing the curtailment of freedom in combating terrorism. 'The expectations of good citizenship are hence related more to compliance and support of the basic needs of society as those are constructed through the lens of security threats' (Ben-Porath, 2006, p. 13).

One would think that the very fundamental freedoms used to make distinctions between individuals living in a liberal democracy from those actions used by terrorists are ironically the freedoms that individuals are willing to forgo in times of crisis (Grayling, 2009). A choice is often given to individuals between the needs of the state before the needs of the individual. And citizenship is often framed as part of one's personal identity (Ben-Porath, 2006, p. 25). The overarching aspect of one's identity is built in to a political identity, one built around one's patriotism and self-sacrifice to one's country. Pledge of Allegiance, flag-waving and other public displays of one's love of one's country are aimed to build 'narrow, unifying and exclusive conceptualizations of national group membership' (*ibid*., p. 25).

A useful distinction might be made at this point between 'patriotism' and 'nationalism'. Li and Brewer (2004) suggest that different manifestations of national identity might arise. Patriotism might be construed as connoting a 'pride and love for country', while nationalism may go further in inciting 'chauvinistic arrogance and desire for dominance in international relations' (p. 728). One attends to the relations among groups within a country in developing cohesive, common values; the other creates a level of supremacy and dominance of a particular set of values that are superior to those defined as less desirable. They argue that in times of threat patriotic tendencies may be warranted to solicit a sense of group identity. That said, such initiatives need to be coupled with a sense of fostering intra-group relationships and an understanding of respect and tolerance. The concern is that such patriotic tendencies will lead to more nationalistic tendencies that limit tolerance to diversity.

The justification for teaching about 9/11 and 7/7 has led many educators to teach about the events to encourage a renewed sense of pride toward one's country. The rationale is that in building such national solidarity we create calm among a citizenry, and a resilience to overcome adversity over such events and not to be unnerved in the face of such tragedies.

Pause for thought

A number of activities are available to commemorate and mark the anniversary of 9/11 for children. The poem below highlights a sense of unity and strength among the American people.

ONE
A 9-11 Remembrance Ceremony
poem by Cheryl Sawyer

Speaker One: As the soot and dirt and ash rained down,
Speaker Two: We became one color.
Speaker One: As we carried each other down the stairs of the burning building
Speaker Three: We became one class.

Speaker One: As we lit candles of waiting and hope
Speaker Four: We became one generation.

Speaker One: As the firefighters and police officers fought their way into the inferno
Speaker Five: We became one gender.

Speaker One: As we fell to our knees in prayer for strength,
Speaker Six: We became one faith.

Speaker One: As we whispered or shouted words of
encouragement,
Speaker Two: We spoke one language.

Speaker One: As we gave our blood in lines a mile long,
Speaker Three: We became one body.

Speaker One: As we mourned together the great loss
Speaker Four: We became one family.

Speaker One: As we cried tears of grief and loss
Speaker Five: We became one soul.

Speaker One: As we retell with pride of the sacrifice of
heroes
Speaker Six: We become one people.

(spoken quickly)

Speaker One: We are
Speaker Two: One color
Speaker Three: One class
Speaker Four: One generation
Speaker Five: One gender
Speaker Six: One faith
Speaker Two: One language
Speaker Three: One body
Speaker Four: One family
Speaker Five: One soul
Speaker Six: One people

ALL: We are The Power of One.
We are United.
We are America.

(permission was graciously granted to use this poem by
Cheryl Sawyer)

- In what ways does the poem provide a sense of reassurance and calm?
- What values are made explicit?
- In times of strife, should schools provide a sense of collective unity and strength? Why or why not?
- Do you think that all individuals would feel included in this poem or will some feel marginalized? Why or why not?

Now let's consider another example in contrast to the previous poem.

The following radio broadcast depicted a Muslim family's experiences in the aftermath of 9/11 and the lessons that were taught to their children and the nationalist identity that was put forth:

Shouting across the Divide
Act One: Which one is not like the others?
www.thisamericanlife.org/play_full.php?play=322&act=1

The book used in the lesson plan depicted the World Trade Center in flames on the cover page and inside had the following statements: 'September 11 was a horrible day. Who did it? We don't know, but we have a clue.'
'Muslims hate Americans.'
'Muslims hate Christians.'
'Muslims believe that anyone who doesn't practice Islam is evil.'
'The Koran teaches war and hate.'

- What narrative is being used to depict the events of 9/11?
- How did the views of the students change in learning this material?
- How did the lessons affect the Muslim girl in her relations with her friends? With her family? Internally?

Finally, compare and contrast the poem 'One' with 'Shouting across the Divide'.

- In what ways can you make out the distinctions between patriotism and nationalism? Is there a notable difference?

- Is there a place for patriotism or nationalism to be taught in schools? Why or why not?
- Is there a moral directive that should be taught in schools regarding patriotism and nationalism or should teachers remain neutral?

Justification two: to understand factors that may influence extremist activities

If the first justification is to create a sense of unity and stability for a nation, justification two takes a proactive stance on attempting to identify and understand the factors that may foster extremist activities. The first part of this claim is to help mitigate and reduce the occurrences of potential extremist threats. The latter part suggests a larger understanding of factors that may encourage further terrorist attacks. Following the 2005 bombings in London, terrorist teaching packs were devised in Calderdale in West Yorkshire inviting pupils to imagine organizing a terrorist attack (Lispett, 2009). The rationale for this approach is that pupils would need to consider the issue from the perspective of the terrorist and consider what makes individuals become extremist in nature. The teaching packs were removed in 2009 after numerous complaints came in that it caused offence. Other attempts to address the factors that lead to terrorist actions include a number of amendments in 2009 to the national UK Graduate Certificate in Secondary Education (GCSE) exams, which contained sections on the 'significance of the Iraq War', asking pupils to consider their views on 'weapons of mass destruction, Saddam Hussein's alleged links to terrorism, Iraq's post-war condition, and the international consequences of the war' (Mansell et al., 2008, p. 16). Similar questions for GCSEs will include 'How effective has terrorism been since 1969?' and considering why people may become terrorists (*ibid.*, p. 16).

Let us consider the first claim accordingly and return to the government booklet, *Learning Together to be Safe* (DCSF, 2008). Recall again the four aims identified in the toolkit:

- Raise **awareness** among schools of the threat from violent extremist groups and the risks for young people.

- Provide **information** about what can cause violent extremism, about preventative actions taking place locally and nationally and about where schools can get additional information and advice.

- Help schools understand the **positive contribution** they can make to empowering young people to create communities that are more resilient to extremism, and **protecting the wellbeing** of particular pupils or groups who may be vulnerable to being drawn into violent extremist activity.

- Provide advice on **managing risks** and responding to incidents locally, nationally or internationally that might have an impact on the school community.

(ibid., p. 5)

The toolkit is targeted for secondary schools and, in particular, school leaders in setting policy for how to prevent extremist activities.

As one reads the *Learning Together to be Safe* toolkit further, it suggests that al-Qaida extremists do not fit a 'typical' profile, nor do they congregate in any one region within the United Kingdom. One must consider the means by which extremists are trained – either internally or in collaboration with international efforts – in attempts to reduce and target these extremist cells. Of the first section that attends to raising awareness about extremist activities, it is interesting to note that only one reference is made to the Irish republican terrorist groups, despite their long-standing terrorist activities in the United Kingdom.

The toolkit calls for an attentiveness to how communities are 'feeling', or observing reactions to a certain terrorist event, and considers the potential for such future events (*ibid.*, p. 13). In this regard, there is both a call to be vigilant towards potential threats, and a proactive stance in changing the extremist discourse that might lead to terrorist activities. Schools are thus to play a key role in interrupting those extremist behaviours in attempting to both disrupt and challenge extremist tendencies and, further, to address grievances that may harbour further resentment among disenfranchised individuals or groups (*ibid.*, p. 13).

To elucidate this point, the toolkit offers examples on how an extremist narrative might be created to persuade and foster extremist thoughts.

Pause for thought

Consider the two examples provided in the toolkit:

a) Al-Qaida and associated groups use a 'single narrative' linking a particular interpretation of history, politics and religion with a number of current grievances – some of which may be quite widely shared by Muslims and non-Muslims alike – to build up a picture of a global conspiracy against Muslims dating back to the crusades. They adopt an extreme interpretation of Islamic teaching that they believe places an obligation to fight and kill to achieve their aims. Most Muslims and the world's leading Islamic scholars reject this interpretation.

b) Far-right extremist ideology provides a hate-based story based on a sense of poverty, discrimination, alienation and threat. It uses local economic and social grievances and distorts analysis of migration, globalization and history and justifies violence to 'protect the indigenous people'. Far-right groups often associate themselves with the Nazis, or other movements such as the Ku Klux Klan. For example 'Combat 18' is the name adopted by a loose collection of violent activists with extreme right-wing neo-Nazi views. '18' represents Hitler, his initials being the first and eighth letters of the alphabet.

- As a teacher, how might one detect these single narratives in the classroom?
- Should a teacher suspect that a student or group of students are sympathetic to these views, how one might disrupt or challenge these narratives?
- In what ways would these narratives influence what or how you taught?
- Is the approach of examining the factors that lead to terrorist activities an effective way of addressing terrorism and extremism in the classroom? Why or why not?

In a similar vein, Richardson (2007) has attempted to identify some of the common identifiers of terrorist organizations and suggests that in order to combat terrorism one must understand its causes. Commonly, terrorist individuals do not see themselves as the aggressor, but as a victim and defender of their beliefs. Numerous interviews with terrorist leaders bring out this point, but it came out clearly when Bin Laden, a well-educated and wealthy man, described his inspiration for the Twin Tower attacks:

> God knows that the plan of striking the towers had not occurred to us, but the idea came to me when things went just too far with the American-Israeli alliance's oppression and atrocities against our people in Palestine and Lebanon. The events that made a direct impression on me were during and after 1982, when America allowed the Israelis to invade Lebanon with the help of its third [Sixth] fleet. They started bombing, killing and wounding many, while others fled in terror ... It was like a crocodile devouring a child, who could do nothing but scream. Does a crocodile understand anything other than weapons? The whole world heard and saw what happened, but did nothing. In those critical moments, many ideas raged inside me, ideas difficult to describe, but they unleashed a powerful urge to reject injustice and a strong determination to punish the oppressors.
>
> As I looked at those destroyed towers in Lebanon it occurred to me to punish the oppressor in kind by destroying towers in America, so that it would have a taste of its own medicine and would be prevented from killing our women and children.
>
> (Bin Laden, 2004, cited in Lawrence, 2005, p. 239)

In this light, we come to understand the motivations that move individuals to take extreme actions against innocent civilians. If acts of war and oppression are committed on their own families, they begin to view their actions as just desert.

In recruiting individuals to the group, Richardson (2007) notes that there is an overwhelming sense of solidarity and camaraderie felt by disenfranchised individuals. Such a unified notion in terrorist groups is notable, and is commonly exacerbated by their surroundings when the surrounding culture glorifies and condones violence (Richardson, 2007, p. 49). Finally, terrorist organizations are those who are part of the minority population who resort to the use of such tactics to gain influence and strength. They usually have a leader who is able to devise a strategic plan and have the resources to follow it through. It then requires the ability of committed followers who have taken up the ideology and are willing to commit their lives to the cause.

Pause for thought

Justification two calls for an examination of the factors that give rise to extremist organizations. This justification is twofold in that it examines the factors that lead to the rise in extremist organizations, and potentially is a safeguard for being attentive to individuals who may be persuaded to join extremist groups.

- To what extent do you think this is an appropriate way in which to address terrorism and extremism in schools?
- Is this an effective way in which to demystify the ideologies to lessen students' interest in joining extremist groups?
- Would you feel comfortable in addressing the factors and causes of terrorism in schools?

Justification three: to be astute in contemporary political affairs

Turf wars about the nature and the aims of various civics curricula have always been prevalent. From the inception of social studies curricula in North America, to the newly created citizenship education subject in England, what one teaches to how one teaches is fraught with vociferous debates. Priorities regarding the extent to which historical and contemporary affairs are addressed are played out in the various legal frameworks and stated objectives, approved textbooks, and in the decisions and judgements about how teachers present and deliver particular content matter.

Given the prevalence of lesson plans and textbook inclusions about 9/11 and 7/7, one of the justifications commonly used for teaching this particular topic is that students must be aware and able to negotiate contemporary political affairs as and when they occur. A thin conception of this might be a descriptive account of the events that play out during the course of the school year. A teacher might contend that students should be informed of current events and require them to find media clippings and accounts of various events, and highlight what is relevant and topical at any given time. A more robust attempt to make students aware of current affairs might entail some critical reflection of the way in which the media portrays and emphasizes certain points to the neglect of others.

This all sounds reasonable and relatively uncontested. Yet, the nature of 9/11 and 7/7 suggest that attending to the complex and multiple perspectives that led up to and may have contributed to these terrorist acts suggests otherwise. Christopher Leahey (2010) contends that the way in which current American social studies textbooks are written conveys a particular message – the myth of war. A particular narrative is provided that highlights the heroics and necessity for certain military action with little counter perspective and insight into a particular event. He notes that, following 9/11, '... the media failed to challenge the Bush Administration's pronouncements, seek out alternative sources of information, provide space for dissenting voices, and portray the dangers and complexity of war' (2010, p. 1). If the media was presenting a particular vantage in favour of military action in Iraq and Afghanistan, how could a teacher address the complexities of the events leading up to and following 9/11? Taking an approach that addresses the complexity of current events might place the teacher in a compromising and precarious position. This is not to be taken lightly. Leahey notes cases where teachers have come under attack for the positions that they took in addressing the war:

> Baker, a senior social studies teacher at Lincoln, Nebraska's East High, was fired for showing his geographic class *Baghdad ER*, which chronicles life inside a combat support hospital in Baghdad; Gutierrez, a 33-year-old social studies teacher from San Fernando High School in California, received negative reviews for teaching about Iraq and having students think critically about war; and Mayer, an elementary school teacher in Bloomington, Indiana, was fired after telling her students, 'I honk for peace' on the eve of the Iraq war.
>
> (*ibid.*, p. 2)

The teachers' alternative perspectives on teaching about the looming wars in Iraq and Afghanistan may have been part of the social studies curriculum to address current affairs, but went beyond what was deemed to be acceptable by the school districts and the constituents of those communities.

Conflicting values and messages are evident. On the one hand, most civics curricula will state that students must be critically reflective, have an awareness of current events, and develop as responsible citizens. Such is reflected in the very formations of how to deliver social studies curricula. The American Historical Association, Committee of Seven met in the late 1800s to articulate this principle:

> The chief object of every experience teacher is to get pupils to think properly … Not an accumulation of information, but the habit of correct thinking … the student who is taught to consider political subjects in school, who is led to look at matters historically, has some mental equipment for a comprehension of the political and social problems that will confront him in everyday life, and has received practical preparation for social adaptation and for forceful participation in civic activities.
>
> (AHA, 1899, p. 18)

The phrasing may have changed, but much of the sentiments still remain in civics curricula. Commonly, the objectives of various social studies, history, citizenship and civic curricula will state that students should be able to have the dispositions necessary to understand, reflect upon and amend the current social and political structures that affect them and their society. The perception is that the current move in American social studies is toward social efficiency: a curriculum structured 'to freeze out alternative visions and create a one-dimensional curriculum supporting social control' (Evans, 2004, p. 177). The claim here is quite stark if such is the case in social studies that narrows and limits the deliberative aspects found in discussing current social and political contemporary affairs.

A call to challenge this narrow conception of social studies is being put forth to resist these trends, particularly in light of and in response to the particular monopolies of textbooks and media in portraying current affairs. In interrupting the positive and selective portrayal of war, Leahey (2010, p. 111) suggests that teachers and students examine textbooks with a critical lens: What is being portrayed? Who is being represented and who is neglected? What is the tone of the text? And what lessons can be learned from the events?

Noam Chomsky (2003) offers a more radical approach in uncovering the complexities surrounding long-term strife, war and terrorism. If we are to be sincere in understanding the deep-rooted anger and long-standing strife between certain peoples and countries (in this case, against the United States and their foreign policies that led up to 9/11), we must understand the role that the United States has taken to create such resentment and hatred. In asking the simple question that might be posed by students, 'Why do they hate us?' Chomsky articulates a few examples of American foreign policy commonly left out of conversations in the American media and the American history textbooks:

> ... that the United States and Britain supported Saddam Hussein right through his worst atrocities, continued to help him develop weapons of mass destruction, didn't do anything to stop him from gassing Kurds or anything else.
>
> (2003, p. 84)

The narrative played out between 'us' and 'them' is told and retold in similar circumstances. When a student asked, 'Why do they hate us?' Michael Sheehan, the Coordinator for Counterterrorism in the State Department between 1998 and 2000, replied, 'They hate us because we love freedom, because we love democracy' (Richardson, 2007, p. 146). The myth of war is put forth as a force between good and evil, and is kept as a single narrative to be played out. Richardson countered, 'What if we learned that, in fact, what they hated was our policies? If we learned that the deployment of our troops in Saudi Arabia was what caused the enmity against us, would this cause you or the administration to re-evaluate the wisdom of our policies?' to which he replied, 'no. We will never let terrorists determine our policies' (*ibid.*, p. 146). The debate was not up for discussion and became a closed matter and non-negotiable. The myth of war is furthered with little opportunity to examine the social and political factors that influence and shape certain events.

To challenge this move toward single narratives, a number of educators contend that we need to examine the political factors that give rise to extremist thought and terrorist activities. This overlaps with justification two in that it not only examines the individual and collective motivations for why individuals join extremist groups, but considers the broader political local and foreign policies that give rise to times of conflict and uncertainty.

Pause for thought

Consider the following excerpts from a lesson plan idea that was used shortly prior to the United States military attack on Iraq in 2003:

A teacher asks the students to read President Bush's State of the Union speech in 2003 and the alleged terrorist threat of Saddam Hussein's Iraq. Have the speech read out to the class and then hold a press conference by the students. Consider some of the following questions for further debate:

- What is an 'outlaw regime'? If the regime goes beyond the parameters of conventional law, what law is Bush referring to?
- Does the history of US–Iraq relations raise any questions about Bush's speech?
- What is Bush's attitude toward the United Nations?
- Can you find any inaccuracies in Bush's speech?
- The president spoke of the possibility of war being 'Forced upon us'. Do you believe that war was forced upon us?
- Also, consider Bush's use of the word 'us'. In what way in this 'our' war? In what way is it not 'our' war?

(Bigelow, 2005, pp. 37–8)

Reflect on this lesson plan approach:

- How safe do you feel in going beyond the formal curriculum and textbook to address contemporary political events and challenge some of the predominant messages offered in the media and by a current administration?

- To what extent do you think that textbooks create a 'myth of war'?
- In what ways might you access information to provide counter positions and perspectives to articulate the complexities of current events?
- In what ways do the media influence current perspectives and events for your students?

Justification four: to promote tolerance, respect and forgiveness

In coming to terms with acts of terror, one might ask whether there is an educational obligation to learn from such events and consider how we might understand such groups' perspectives and even come to some form of reconciliation.

The popularity of Richardson's terrorism lectures was notable following 9/11. What had become a long eccentric area of research and personal interest (given her upbringing in Northern Ireland during the Troubles[5]), Richardson notes how many of the individuals wanted to understand why terrorists do what they do. One of her assignments for the term was for each student to choose a particular terrorist group, and understand their mission, and become fully aware of their activities – simply, to become fully immersed in the ethos of a particular terrorist group (2007, p. xviii). She describes the phenomena that tended to occur as follows:

Almost without exception, the student would start his presentation (and they were predominantly males) by saying something

---

[5] The Troubles was a period of conflict in Northern Ireland dating from the late 1960s and is arguably suggested to have ended with the Belfast 'Good Friday' Agreement of 1998. The ongoing conflict often arose between the political status of Northern Ireland in the United Kingdom. Violence and terrorist attacks were common arising from both the Irish Republican Army and that of the Ulster loyalist paramilitary groups.

like "well, all those other groups are terrorist groups, but if
you really look at the ETA [Euskadi Ta Askatasuna, an armed
Basque nationalist and separatist organization], or IRA [Irish
Republican Army] or Shining Path, or whichever movement
he had chosen, you discover that they are not really terrorists.
Do you know what happened to them, or do you know what
they do for the poor? Or do you know about their cultural
programs?

(*ibid.*, p. xviii)

The point here is that these students had a more nuanced perspective
of the particular group they had followed. The aim overlaps
with the previous justifications to understand the factors that
lead to extremist organizations. Understanding political contexts
these individuals face – that of the 'other' – someone who is not
perceived as 'evil' or 'fanatical' or simply 'alien', but to make aware
of the political conditions gives individuals a more nuanced understanding of why certain individuals resort to extreme measures. As
such, it requires an understanding and acknowledgement of the
social and political conditions to which these groups are able to
gain followers that fuel their extremism.

In coming to understand the 'other', the aim is to break down the
barriers that may lead to continued strife and struggle. Ben-Porath
(2006) suggests an expansive education that overlaps with many
of the tenets found in multicultural curricula. In times of war and
long-term conflict it is difficult see how one might begin to move an
educational programme toward the aims of peace and democracy.
The overarching principles involve:

Learning to bridge rifts, to overcome hatred, to take the other's
perspective, to recognize other historical narratives are all
potential parts of both multicultural and expansive education.
In both cases they must be socially and culturally contextualized
if they are to remain relevant and responsive.

(Ben-Porath, 2006, p. 95)

In coming to understand the other's perspective, we hope to
break down stereotypes and single narrative myths that build
resentment and alienation. And while the intent is not to make
opposing sides necessarily agree on fundamental beliefs, it is to

find how one can live together and 'accept differing perspectives on salient social matters' (*ibid.*, p. 95). Social recognition is essential to one's identity and self- worth; conversely, the absence or 'misrecognition of others' can create incredible damage and hardship on both one's own identity and the resentment towards others (Taylor, 1994, p. 25).

Acknowledgement and understanding of others is one way in which to come to terms with terrorist events. Others suggest that if one is to move forward towards some reconciliation, we need to move beyond this to a notion of 'forgiveness'. Such is the sentiment of Archbishop Tutu's book, *No Future without Forgiveness* (1999), which suggests that forgiveness is a key component to reconciliation between warring factions. If forgiveness is required to move us toward a more hopeful goal, Patricia White (2007) considers whether this disposition ought to be taught in citizenship education. While White is cautious about political forgiveness where it is unclear which groups of membership must show remorse – i.e. those political leaders who commit the crimes – to those who are willing to forgive – the actual victims or those indirectly affected by the violation – there may be pause for considering aspects of forgiveness after certain human violations have been committed. While the notion of forgiveness may not require reconciliation where victims are willing or able to completely forgive the perpetrators (Morton, 2004, cited in White, 2007, p. 12), one might consider other aspects of forgiveness that are both attainable and useful. A public acknowledgement that gives victims a public space for their stories to be heard and their grief to be noted may provide solace. Such public acknowledgement might include 'the impact on the bereaved and inured, remembrance and commemoration, debates about forgiveness, expressions of regret, apology and symbolic events, understanding the role of amnesties, prisoner releases, alongside concepts of restorative and transitional justice' (Smith, 2005, p. 385). In furthering this, permanent institutions whose role to protect and secure fundamental human rights serve an essential function for developing ways to create stability in post-war conflicts (White, 2007, p. 13). White suggests that the educational role then might be for individuals 'to *understand* these institutions as instantiations of the values of respect for persons, justice and truth-seeking' (*ibid.*, p. 13).

Pause for thought

TED (Technology Entertainment and Design) Talks are a global set of conferences run by a not-for-profit institution to encourage and spread innovative ideas and design. Speakers are given a maximum of 18 minutes in which to convey their idea or innovation. In one such talk, '9/11 healing: The mothers who found forgiveness, friendship', two mothers talk about their tragedies and healing process. Phyllis Rodrguez's son was killed in the World Trade Center attacks, while Aicha el-Wafi's son was convicted in playing a terrorist role on those attacks and is serving a life sentence. In this talk, they advocate a message of forgiveness and respect.

Watch the video:
9/11 healing: The mothers who found forgiveness, friendship
www.ted.com/talks/lang/eng/9_11_healing_the_mothers_who_found_forgiveness_friendship.html

Consider the extent to which schools might be able or willing to teach about tolerance, respect and forgiveness after terrorist attacks have occurred.

- Is it possible for teachers to provide a balanced view of the perspectives of others in light of terrorist activities committed?
- Should a teacher remain neutral in such discussions about reconciliation or forgiveness?
- In what ways might a teacher find it difficult to teach about tolerance, respect and forgiveness?
- Is this an appropriate or effective way in which to talk about terrorist events? Why or why not?
- Toleration and respect are terms that are commonly written into citizenship and social studies curricula. Should forgiveness also be included as part of citizenship education?

Conclusion

It is clear that a great spectrum exists in the justifications used to teach about extremism and terrorism. The approach one wishes to take (or avoid completely), will have considerable ramifications. Vigilance against potential terrorist threats will have different objectives than teaching about forgiveness. Other justifications may be complementary and overlapping. Teaching about the factors that persuade individuals to join extremist groups may require an understanding of the political circumstances that fuel such organizations. Interestingly, the number of readily available lesson plans, textbook explanations or policy and curriculum documents does little to provide teachers and schools with critically negotiating the multiple, and often contradicting, aims.

In order to find a way through this incredibly complex and emotionally sensitive topic, the next chapter will turn our attention to the construction of knowledge in the classroom in further detail. In unpacking this debate, we will then consider the extent to which teachers should remain neutral in such controversial and sensitive topics.

Further reading

I have highlighted four different approaches that are commonly used in teaching terrorism and extremism in schools. You may now wish to consider a number of websites that offer lesson plans and suggested activities and reflect on where the emphases lie and what is omitted:

www.facinghistory.org is a not-for-profit organization providing educational workshops and supplementary resources in combating bigotry and nurturing democracy. Although its original mandate was to provide a thorough examination into the events that led to the Holocaust, it does focus on recent events attending to issues of genocide and mass violence. It has produced a number of suggested activities to address the issues surrounding 9/11.

www.scholastic.com/911day/ Scholastic book publishers are one of the largest book distributors to students and educators across North America. They provide books, lesson plans, teaching resources, curriculum and leadership guidance, parental and children's suggested tips for guided reading. A special section has been devoted to developing and sharing various lesson ideas and teaching resources for the tenth anniversary of 9/11 in America.

http://pbskids.org/itsmylife/emotions/sept11/   The Public Broadcasting System (PBS) is a television channel funded by the Corporation for Public Broadcasting. In addition to television programming targeted for kids (PBS kids), they offer an online interactive website for supplementary activities and games. One portion of this website is devoted to children's perspectives on 9/11 in dealing with it emotionally.

www.socialstudies.org/resources/moments The National Council of Social Studies has put forth a number of lesson plans on terrorism and extremism. They offer guiding principles in which to address in the social studies curricula, along with suggested activities to attend to those guiding principles.

http://future.state.gov/educators/lessons/ The US Department of State for Youth, in collaboration with American social studies educators, has developed a resource package equipped with video clips, instructional activities and narratives stories in addressing terrorism.

www.teachingcitizenship.org.uk/ The Association for Citizenship Teaching in England and Wales provides resources and support to educators who teach citizenship education in the United Kingdom. One its common themes is how to address terrorism within the overarching objectives set out in the citizenship curriculum.

www.education.gov.uk/search/results?q=terrorism   The Department of Education in England and Wales provides a number of publications, videos and resources particularly related to citizenship (and the topic of terrorism). Specific articles related to the threat of terrorism and how to teach about key concepts in citizenship education are readily available on this website.

CHAPTER THREE

The Social Construction of Knowledge in the Classroom

If the way in which we approach and justify the topic of terrorism in the classroom is varied and contested, it is useful to step back and consider the ways in which knowledge is constructed both in schools and society. How we approach a topic is laden with one's presuppositions, beliefs, values and judgements about what one should or should not include. One might consider overt cases that incite religious hatred or indoctrination to be unacceptable and to be condemned. We might, for instance, have little trouble in condemning the textbooks that were funded by United States Agency for International Development (USAID) and created in the mid-1990s for children across Afghanistan and Pakistan that had explicit messages promoting the jihad. The teaching of the alphabet had specific references to war and violence – for example, 'K is for Kalashnikov' and pictures depicting child soldiers – leaving little room for possible acceptance of such explicit messages of hatred and violence (El Eldroos, 2011). Yet, how knowledge is constructed and conveyed, both formally in the curriculum and informally, arguably has an impact on our perspectives and judgements towards certain beliefs and individuals. How we name and describe certain events are all value laden. In this chapter, I wish to consider the ways in which knowledge is constructed and presented. I will begin with the narrowing of debate towards extremist rhetoric in public discourse. I will then move on to the way in which political events and discussions are depicted as opposing forces, highlighting the extremes of the debate, rather than articulating the complexity and nuances within the process of deliberation. If the political pundits and politicians leave little room for negotiation and compromise, it is of no surprise that the way in which the media and pop culture plays up the contested battle between 'good' and 'evil' is proliferated. In the final section I return to schools, where I consider how both external and internal factors influence the nature of the debate and the construction of knowledge in a formal setting.

Shutting down the debate: the language between 'us' and 'them'

In most liberal democracies, fundamental freedoms of speech, association, religion and conscience are protected either within Constitutions or embedded within the legal traditions and precedents. Although discretion as to the parameters of such freedoms may be defined between and within countries (for instance, that of hate speech) (Dworkin, 2002), the underpinning principles of a democracy are defined by these fundamental rights. Further, in setting up civil society that protects these individual freedoms is an implicit understanding that it is beneficial and acceptable for individuals to be able to foster their own sense of identity as part of their flourishing as individuals. Although fundamental freedoms and fostering a sense of identity are integral to a vibrant democracy, at times a delicate balancing act can come into play.

The notion of allowing individuals the ability to foster their own sense of identity without fear of reprisal or punishment is clearly laid out by Will Kymlicka (1989, 1995). If democracies are to allow for individuals to decide how they wish to lead their life in accordance to their own beliefs and values, as part of developing their identity, this may entail protecting their right to cultural membership. Kymlicka states: '(1) that cultural membership has a more important status in liberal thought than is explicitly recognized – that is, that the individuals who are an unquestionable part of the liberal moral ontology are viewed as individual members of a particular cultural community, for whom cultural membership is an important good; and (2) that members of minority cultural communities may face particular kinds of disadvantages with respect to the good of cultural membership, disadvantages whose rectification requires and justifies the provision of minority rights' (*ibid.*, p. 162). This claim does hold resonance. You can imagine, for instance, how superficial the protection of individual fundamental freedoms would be if such rights would not entail the ability of individuals to foster shared beliefs and values with other like-minded individuals. One of the benefits of having such associations is the way in which communities have the potential to develop their own self-worth and identity through these communal bonds (Gereluk, 2006).

Few individuals would contest the notion that part of developing one's identity requires relations with others. The difficulty lies in when a particular shared identity envelops one's perspective to the exclusion or impairment of others. In the book *Identity and Violence*, Sen (2006) wrestles with the fine balance of being allowed to create a sense of identity with others without it inciting hatred or resentment. Very simply, 'the incitement to ignore all affiliation and loyalties other than those emanating from one restrictive identity can be deeply delusive and also contribute to social tension and violence' (*ibid.*, p. 21). The statement could clearly be targeted to those groups that have extremist and fundamentalist beliefs. However, the same might be true in others' reactions to and resistance to those who do not fit in to the mainstream. We get into an awkward 'he said', 'she said' fight of creating two opposing factions each unwilling to listen to the other's perspectives.

One might challenge this notion of identity though. We have multiple associations and plural ways in which we create identities through our varied associations. We might define and be defined by our profession, our familial relationships, our ethnicity or race, our hobbies or interests. These multiple communities must surely influence the way in which we construct and see ourselves as persons. True, but individuals might not necessarily give the same weight or value to all of their various associations regarding their identity. Some aspects of our association may simply hold more value than others. My interest of playing the violin may be a significant part of my identity, but my political and religious affiliations often influence my thoughts and actions in both my personal and professional life. Two things become apparent then: 1) individuals belong to multiple communities that shape their personal identities; 2) each of these associations will most certainly not have equal standing or import. That form of deliberation requires an individual's form of reasoning and choice in prioritizing and making value judgements about their life (*ibid.*, p. 29). Commonly, individuals are viewed within various identifiers that stereotype and confine people to single identities based on their race, religion or culture. Shortly following the 7/7 bombings in London, a review was conducted by the Department for Education and Skills (DfES), headed by Sir Keith Ajegbo, to examine 'diversity issues', particularly considering how British cultural and social history could be incorporated into citizenship lessons at the secondary level. *Diversity and Curriculum Review* (DfES, 2007), commonly referred to as the Ajegbo Report, noted that not enough was being done in schools to promote the 'Diversity for All' objectives for pupils in their schools; instead, pupils were reduced to simple stereotypes by the ways in which their identity was constructed in the curriculum and in the classroom:

> While it is important to understand another person's religion, ethnicity and culture in order to appreciate more fully who they are, it is then simplistic to define them by one of these alone. Stereotyping often goes further than that. Many African Caribbean boys, for instance, feel defined in school just by their blackness; a crude popular definition of what it is to be a Muslim is now developing; Gypsy, Roman and Traveller children are often 'invisible' in the wider community; working class white pupils are all too easily stereotyped as 'chavs'.
>
> (*ibid.*, p. 29)

One of the main conclusions of the Report is that schools need to be limited to identity and diversity discussions based solely on religion, but need to be inclusive of a much more holistic concept of identity explicitly discussed and explored within the citizenship curriculum.

If the starting assumption is that we create identities through our associations, it is also clear that our identities are created by the ways in which others view us. How we are perceived, acknowledged, understood and respected influence our own sense of identity, not only internally among members of a community, but in how we are perceived externally. Consider yet another example that has segregated individuals in a society. The legislation on banning all ostentatious religious symbols in French schools in 2004 created much public debate not only about the place of religion in the civic republican traditions of France, but more fundamentally brought out key central debates about the stability of civil society. Bowen contends that the legislation was particularly aimed at curtailing the hijab:

> The debate and votes perplexed many observers. French public figures seemed to blame the headscarves for a surprising range of France's problems, including anti-Semitism, Islamic fundamentalism, growing ghettoization in the poor suburbs, and the breakdown of order in the classroom.
>
> (2007, p. 1)

The identification and perception of the French nationalism brought conjured images of the oppressed Islamic woman and the undermining of the French republican traditions of liberty, equality and fraternity. Yet, in implementing such legislation, it created a new form of identity based on resistance and backlash between the Islamic communities and the traditional 'French' communities. The chasm between 'French' and 'foreigner' was furthered in this oppositional stance (Gereluk, 2008).

The artificial creation of dualism between an 'us' and 'them' scenario does little to foster the dispositions of a democracy. Yet, there is an increasing prevalence of the language that limits an alternative perspective and closes off debate. Much of the language used to portray 9/11 and 7/7 in the general public conveyed little attempt to understand *why* something may have occurred, to an emotive stance to be fought back, heroes to be erected, villains to be sought, and justice and freedom to prevail:

> In the aftermath of the events of September 11, through public rhetoric, an act of terror became a war, the Bush presidency was

ratified, New York became America's city, with Rudy Giuliani as "mayor of the world." Patriotism became consumerism, dissent was discouraged, and Americans became students, newly schooled in strategic geography
and Islam.

(Silberstein, 2002, p. xi)

In the lead up to the invasion of Afghanistan, the political rhetoric was plentiful. Negative phrases quickly unfolded to describe and justify an invasion. Terms such as 'acts of evil'; 'the war on terror', 'an enemy', 'an attack on America' and 'this generation's "Pearl Harbour"' were used liberally in cultivating hatred and a resounding solidarity to call to (violent) action.

If the negative phrases did little to create a unified response from citizens, patriotic and heroic messages were conveyed to create a sense that it would be (un)patriotic to question the actions of the state. Part of the rhetoric was to (re)create a national identity, one that was unwavering and unquestioning (Silberstein, 2002), set up with a level of certainty that only a traitor would challenge. With little exception, the language used through the use of sound bites conveyed a clear message of retribution and justice against the Islamic terrorists.

The use of language to create certainty and a dichotomy between 'good' and 'evil' puts us on a troublesome path towards 'extremist rhetoric' (Gutmann, 2007). Such language degrades complex issues and difficult scenarios with little opportunity for deliberation, reasoned debate on substantively central issues. While such language may make for better public media ratings, or more rousing applause from a public rally, it denigrates the democratic discourse and narrowing of understanding. And while the general citizenry who listen to this dualistic language may not be extremist in nature, the extremist rhetoric has some troublesome implications. 'First, it tends toward single-mindedness on any given issue. Second, it passionately expresses certainty about the supremacy of its perspective' (*ibid.*, p. 71). Those who disagree are held in disrepute and to be viewed as suspicious. We cannot trust those who may disagree or provide countering positions. We create enemies within our own citizenry who show dissent. In effect, citizens are encouraged to the lowest common denominator of democratic deliberation of that of 'lemmings'. We listen to the cursory debates provided, reuse the phrases used repeatedly in the political rhetoric, and show our sympathies for the 'winning' side. It becomes a real-life example of George Orwell's premise in his book, *1984*, where the narrowing and skewing of language inhibits conversation and limits those who contest and challenge the rhetoric.

The danger with narrowing such language between two camps – West and non-West (particularly that of Islam) – is that potential exists for non-Western individuals to consider themselves as 'the other' and create a 'reactive identity' (Sen, 2006, p. 91). If dualisms are created to pit one against the other, then a tendency may occur to consider themselves primarily as being different from Western values, and perpetuate and foster extremist views. Tariq Ramadan has argued vehemently against this oppositional discourse that is created between the West and non-West and notes the potential ramifications for such false dichotomies:

> ... the overwhelming majority of the world's Muslims – particularly western Muslims – recognise the achievements of western societies, while at the same time claiming the right to determine for themselves the parameters of their identity, the nature and extent of their religious practices, and their spiritual and moral convictions. Seen from this perspective, criticism and rejection of the west are linked only to a refusal to accept political, economic or cultural domination.
>
> (Ramadan, 2010)

Being hostile to those practices that have subjugated a group of individuals due to foreign policies is much different than being hostile to the fundamental principles of liberty and equality. Making such oversimplifications does little to enter into a rational deliberate debate. Instead of trying to create a sense of shared values and commonality between groups, we divide and create resistance between groups. We further distort history as if it was the West that championed values of liberty, and that Islamic ideals must be hostile to such views (Sen, 2006, p. 84). In creating this oppositional discourse, it undermines 'the support for democracy or liberty in the non-Western world' (*ibid.*, p. 93). Islam is commonly misrepresented by the West as anti-Christian, non-European, and fundamentalist (Said, 1993).

Now, one might be sceptical at this point and contend that the political discourse was warranted given the gravity of the event against innocent civilians, and the appropriate response was for a unified front against terrorism. The point I wish to make is that the ability to take a reasoned stance on any given issue is limited in the ways in which conversations block out certain views. It might be the case that having had such a reasoned and thoughtful discussion regarding the terrorist attacks may still have warranted an attack on Afghanistan. However, not having the ability to have such a discussion due to the extremist rhetoric used in the first course is what is problematic here. The closing of the debate in the first instance through the narrowing and certainty of language undermines the basis of the principles upon which a democracy is supposed to be founded. The point is simply this: it is possible to have a thoughtful, reasoned understanding of a debate, and still feel that you are within your means of agreeing with the dominant perspective. The critical element is that one must first be allowed to enter into the debate.

Pause for thought

We have seen the narrowing of deliberative discourse before. The McCarthy era (approximately from the late 1940s to the late 1950s) was infamous for its witch hunts for those who were perceived to be sympathetic to left ideologies – most notably communists. Many innocent Americans were fired and charged with much haste and little justification to warrant the allegations or the charges.

Consider the ways in which language is used to create a false dichotomy between central debates regarding:
- abortion
- evolution and creationism
- immigration
- faith and reason.
- How are terms used to convey an 'either/or' scenario?
- Is there a way in which one can resist extremist rhetoric?
- What are the possible ramifications if you counter such opinions?
- Can you think of any further debates that narrow the debate between 'us' and 'them'?

Political (lack of) discourse: politicians, news correspondents, and political debates

If the public debate has created a discourse that limits the complexity of central issues such as terrorism, the role of the media and news correspondents, political debates and politicians has further exacerbated the problem with little exception. Even prior to the events of 9/11 and 7/7, the way in which the media portrayed and discussed a singular identity of the 'Other' and those not of the 'West' was notable (Richardson, 2001). How we name and describe events, label and reduce groups of individuals to single descriptors, and limit the ability to challenge such discourses was prevalent both prior to and following the terrorist attacks. One need not look far in the way British Muslims are portrayed in England, or French Muslims in France to suggest that more is at play in placing them as 'foreign' and 'hostile' to those of British or French ancestry. In a letter published in the *Daily Telegraph* in 1997, the comments signify much sentiment in English public:

> If immigrants will not adapt to our ways in public life – as Christians readily do in Muslim countries – the future looks grim. And if veils become commonplace in Britain, villains could resort to them instead of the less concealing stocking mask. Add a loose robe and you would never know the wearer's sex.
> (Mona McNee, *Daily Telegraph*, 5 December 1997, cited in Richardson, 2001, p. 221)

The hostility is marked, but it conveys a number of messages about the perceptions of Islamic communities and the notable Islamophobia (*ibid.*, p. 222). The argumentative tone of the letter implies that there is one type of Islamic faith; Muslims are considered and viewed as one group. The second aspect is that Muslims are foreigners and not considered part of the British milieu. The perception is that Muslims are 'immigrants' rather than potentially having been born and raised in England. Third is that Muslims have different and hostile views, and that the proper course is for them to assimilate to the British way of life. The reference to Muslims' 'different ways' is to be viewed with suspicion and cause for concern. Conversely, in the following sentence, Muslims should be contrasted to Christians, who are both flexible and adaptable. Finally, if Muslims do not fit the British mould, then the future of the British society is at stake.

The letter may not have been the expressed views of the publication. However, John Richardson's (2001, 2009) extensive linguistic analysis on media portrayal of British Muslims in newspapers conveys similar anti-Islamic messages. Common trends occurred when Richardson tracked the usage of British Muslim news stories. Commonly, the portrayal of negative news items of Muslims were of an international rather than local nature. It was noted that over the period 1993–97, of the 8,075 articles written about Muslims published in *The Guardian* and *The Times*, only 1,224 were about British Muslims (Poole, 2000, p. 4, cited in Richardson, 2001, p. 228). Further, rarely were British Muslims provided a voice, but were passive participants in the events unfolding. Little commentary was given by British Muslims. Interpretations and events were presented from the newspaper's perspective with little counter input. Language depicted in the newspapers created further dualisms toward extremist rhetoric. Overwhelmingly, language created a division between the 'British and 'non-British' by indicating how Muslims were 'separate', 'inferior' or the 'enemy' (*ibid.*, pp. 230–3). The implications of this language are telling. It creates a dualism that divides, oppresses and marginalizes those who do not fit within the dominant Western ideologies.

If the media presented a certain bias that created a certain bias, political debates in the media prove little better. A common tactic in television news networks is to pit two opposing political pundits to discuss an issue. Rarely do debates attend to the complexity of an issue, but exacerbate and divide between two opposing camps. The point is not to find common ground or compromise, but to divide and create further barriers to any issue.

Let us turn to one such recurring news story that occurred on the show *The O'Reilly Factor*, where O'Reilly interviewed one of the 9/11 victim's sons, Jeremy Glick.

O'REILLY: But who is this guy, really? Well, on this programme, Glick said President [George W.] Bush and his father [former President George H. W. Bush] were responsible for his [Glick's] father's death. He said George W. Bush pulled off a coup to get elected. He implied the USA itself was a terrorist nation. And he called his father's death at the hands of an al-Qaeda 'alleged assassination'. He said America itself was responsible for the 9/11 attack because it is an imperialistic, aggressive nation. Glick was dismissed from *The Factor* because he was completely off the wall. Security actually had to take the guy out of the building, he was that out of control.

(20 July 2004 edition of FOX News Channel's *The O'Reilly Factor*)

Yet, when you go back to the original transcripts between O'Reilly and Glick, aired 4 February 2003, you see what Glick had originally said:

[O]ur current president now inherited a legacy from his father and inherited a political legacy that's responsible for training militarily, economically, and situating geopolitically the parties involved in the alleged assassination and the murder of my father and countless of thousands of others.

(3 February 2003 edition of FOX News Channel's *The O'Reilly Factor*)

How quotes are used and misinterpreted is part of the task in creating extremist rhetoric. Instead of attempting to understand and deliberate the sensitive and contested nature of the topic, the news reporter distorts and manipulates the conversation to put forth a particular view. Although Glick's comments may have been both deliberately provocative and may have incited heated debate, O'Reilly uses sound bites and distorts Glick's comments to make him appear both unsound and extremist in his thoughts.

Major news outlets proved to be similarly extremist and titillating in their run-up to the invasion of Iraq. Leahey (2010) notes the ways in which major news outlets marked the looming hours before the invasion of Iraq:

MSNBC ran "Countdown Iraq," an electronic clock showing the hours Saddam Hussein had to comply with President Bush's directive to leave Iraq. By prefacing its half-hour segments with the slogan "showdown Iraq," CNN treated the pending invasion as a Western gunfight. NBC's "Target Iraq," CBS's "America at

War," and NBC's "War in Iraq" packaged the commodity to be consumed, not as a critical event worth of a national discourse.

(*ibid.*, p. 2)

Little debate or deliberation ensued. The news sensationalized the event as a movie to be watched while eating popcorn at a theatre. Similar theatrical vignettes played out on news streams in the spring that year of Iraqi citizens rejoicing in the streets while the statue of Saddam Hussein was toppled and of President Bush declaring a premature victory in Iraq on 1 May 2003.

However, it hasn't only been the right-wing agenda that largely created this extremist rhetoric; the left has had its share of divisive extremist rhetoric created in the media as well. During the 2004 election campaign, Moveon.org developed a television advert comparing President George W. Bush to Hitler and the Nazis. The commercial depicted images of Hitler and the rights of the Nazi regime, with recordings and images of Nazi Germany. The advert ended with a visual image of Bush raising his hand to take the oath of office, with the statement: 'A nation warped with lies. Lies fuel fear. Fear fuels aggression. Invasion. Occupation. What were war crimes in 1945 is foreign policy in 2003' (as cited in Gutmann, 2007, p. 73). Again, the message is unwavering and extremist in tone. It portrays those in favour of Republican policies as being sympathetic to that of the Nazi regime.

Political extremist rhetoric continues to be a common strategy used in party politics. From the first days after the attack, the rallying cry to attack the enemy and restore justice was a common theme. George W. Bush led the war cry:

Tonight we are a country awakened to danger and called to defend freedom. Our grief has turned to anger, and anger to resolution. Whether we bring our enemies to justice, or bring justice to our enemies, justice will be done ...

Americans are asking, why do they hate us? They hate what they see right here in this chamber – a democratically elected government. Their leaders are self-appointed. They hate our freedoms – our freedom of religion, our freedom of speech, our freedom to vote and assemble and disagree with each other.

(Address to the Joint Session of Congress, 20 September 2001)

It is little wonder that citizens grew fearful of the 'Other' and developed a firm resolve toward retribution and justice. Those who critiqued and challenged the rhetoric that was presented and put forth in the public sphere were ridiculed and attacked as unpatriotic. No clearer was this made than on 20 September 2001, when President Bush stated, 'Every nation in every region has a decision to make. Either you are with us, or you are with the terrorists.' France's stance of not entering the Iraq War was met with resound disapproval from the American citizenry. Tourism to France declined, and any reference to France would be changed.

Similar rhetoric was found in England from then Prime Minister Tony Blair. In his last speech made to the party conference, Blair reiterated his stance and support for England's role in invading Iraq:

> This terrorism isn't our fault. We didn't cause it. It's not the consequence of foreign policy.
> It is an attack on our way of life. It is global. It has an ideology. We will not win until we shake ourselves free of the wretched capitulation to the propaganda of the enemy that somehow we are the ones responsible.
>
> (Tony Blair, September 2006)

Again, the clear message is that the terrorists have nothing in common with us, and are against our fundamental beliefs and values which must be defended. As a nation, we must be united and determined to stop the enemy.

One might argue and state that such certainty is required in times of instability and fear. The unified and unwavering messages of politicians may have created a calm and resilience among its citizenry. One might further suggest that anger is an appropriate response given the nature of the attacks on a large innocent group of individuals. If an act causes gross injustice and tragedy, perhaps anger and solidarity are necessary to uphold such democratic freedoms. Patricia White (2011) considers whether anger is an appropriate disposition in a democracy. If, for example, individuals feel as if their human rights abuses, a violation of fundamental freedoms or a sense of security are being undermined, perhaps anger is required. But here, White considers whether that anger in and of itself might be an appropriate emotional response, but more importantly, whether channelling such anger in a certain direction may be required. One might well consider that remorse and anger against the enemy would be inappropriate if random beatings occurred on anyone considered to be a Muslim. We might, however, consider turning any initial anger and sympathy toward such extremist rhetoric, and consider, 'Who is saying who is angry and who is the audience for the utterance? What is the purpose?' (*ibid.*, p. 20). Anger is a common response that resonates with much of the public citizenry; yet, creating an unchallenging and single narrative on such an issue does little to provide a robust understanding of *how* to channel such anger.

Given the extremist rhetoric and single narratives offered in political debates in the media and in party politics, an interesting development has occurred in media, with political satire television shows, most notably *The Daily Show* in the United States. Although explicitly a satirical political comedy, much of the interviews conducted provide counter narratives and critiques of the ways in which news is presented in mainstream political news networks. It plays on the narrow, superficial portrayal of news coverage, by reporting on recent news stories, political events and national and international politicians.

Pause for thought

Use the following questions to think about how media and politicians shape and convey what they deem to be 'newsworthy'.

- List some phrases you have heard in the media regarding 9/11 and 7/7. What words are commonly used over and over again?
- What visual representations are used when news stories about terrorism are broadcast?
- What aspects of terrorism are ignored?
- Can you think of any news programmes or political debates that do not create opposing camps?
- On any given night, note how much time each news story receives on any given news hour? How much time is devoted to: local news; national news; international news; human interest stories; sports?

Name that villain: media and pop culture

If extremist rhetoric and the creation of dualisms are rife in the public sphere in society, they are clearly exacerbated and played out in movies and literature. With few exceptions, the basis of a story is based on a protagonist, the main character, and the antagonist, the opponent or rival character in a story. The antagonist is often portrayed in a negative light, morally corrupt, with destructive means against the protagonist. The protagonist's main intent is to overcome the evil actions or obstacles that the antagonist plots. It is the battle between the 'good guys' and 'bad guys', and while there are notable exceptions where the roles are reversed, the general templates for storylines are based around this battle.

So it is of little surprise that one can easily look to movies to see how stereotypes and archetypes of characters often parallel the public mood and anxiety on a political level. Following the Second World War up until the early 1990s saw a proliferation of movies in which Soviets, East Germans, Chinese, North Koreans and those with Communist sympathies were to be loathed and feared. The development of the antagonist character is given great biographical detail in order to engage and connect with the viewer's inner anxieties and fears. A list of attributes and mental descriptors are created and exaggerated. Overall appearance and outstanding physical traits often mark the antagonist, including: dirty appearance; defining facial markers; symbolic clothing that may be reminiscent of a political or religious background; and their decrepit moral and ethical standards, temperaments, and (lack of) virtuous qualities.

This is not limited to adult movies, but is ever present in the very young to the very old. Disney's *Aladdin* (1993) received sharp criticism from Islamic and Arab communities for the stereotypical portrayal of Muslims and Arabs. The opening scenes show the Arabs as conniving and dirty, hustling in the markets, veiled women, thieving children, and generally a scene of chaos and disorder. In one of the opening lines of the first song in the early release of the movie, it sang, 'they cut off your ear if they don't like your face'; upon receiving much protest, Disney executives rewrote the particular line (Ward, 2007).

The early television cartoon series of *Rocky and Bullwinkle* had the arch villains of Boris Badenov ('bad enough') and Natalie Fatale (based on the concept of Femme Fatale), two Eastern bloc spies with thick Russian accents and stereotypical spy appearance. The protagonists, in contrast, were iconic American symbols of Rocky the flying squirrel and Bullwinkle a loveable moose, residing in Frostbite Falls, Minnesota, heart of the American north-west (based on the city of International Falls, Minnesota). The long-running success of the show was marked from 1959–1973, with a tried and true plot structure of Rocky and Bullwinkle stopping the arch villains who continually attempted to attack and destroy the American way of life.

Crude stereotypes of the archetypical antagonist often follow a similar template. The Communist villain – be it Soviet, East German or Chinese – often would exhibit a rough, sometimes scarred, face. The characters often wore black, brown or grey uniforms, paralleling many of the authoritarian uniform regimes. The living conditions in which the antagonists were portrayed often showed rural (backward), bleak (run-down buildings) or harsh conditions (e.g Siberia). They showed the regimes of which the antagonists preside being inflexible, brutal and unforgiving to citizens (often including a cruel treatment of their own authoritarian regimes to their own antagonists).

With the reduced strength and power of the Soviet regimes and the fall of the Berlin Wall in 1989, a new enemy was sought. The Communist regime did not exert the same threat or fear as it once did during the McCarthy and Cold War periods up until shortly after the Reagan years. A new enemy had to be found: cue the Middle Eastern/ Muslim villain. The archetypal stereotype for the antagonist would now look and feel as follows. Bustling street markets with snake charmers, yelling men, veiled women and pandemonium would set the scene for many a movie. Increasing terrorist movies would emerge with an underlying theme that violent, wife-beating men are willing to die and become martyrs. And behind every dark-looking person lurks a potential terrorist (Ward, 2007). The social and economic conditions run a parallel theme to that of the Cold War settings: harsh, hot climates in backward conditions, where poverty and repression are pervasive among its citizenry. Women are seen as powerless and docile, and men are depicted as tyrannical. With few exceptions, the hope is that 'good' will prevail over 'evil'. The classic James Bond movies developed this template over 40 years, with the main character, James Bond, playing a savvy, debonair spy, martini in hand and beautiful girl by his side, taking on the political villains of the world who attempt to undermine the fundamental freedoms that exist in the Western world.

One might contend that such movies are parodies and should

be taken in such a light. Yet, the concern here is the barrage of messages, symbols and perceptions that create a gorge between 'us' and 'them', distorting the complexity of an issue regarding relations between nations, groups and individuals. If this is the case regarding the general adult population, one might easily conjecture that such an effect would be far greater in children. Few would challenge the claim that children's cognitive capacity to reason, critically reflect and negotiate information are continually developing and maturing; as such, controversial material will be difficult to comprehend in the best of circumstances and presenting it through a distorted lens only exacerbates the problem. It further creates yet another obstacle in coming to understand an issue when preconceived notions and prejudices are formed through both deliberate and unintentional images and messages found in media and pop culture. One may easily observe these phenomena by noting how children are influenced by the clothing industries and the labels that identify children's identity. If children are persuaded by the commercialization and marketization found in the public sphere, surely this would spill onto the messages and images that they receive through various modes of media.

Pause for thought

Consider the two categories of movie villains listed below. Notice the dates the movies were released and the changing nature of the antagonist in each of the movies.

Communist or former Soviet Bloc villain	Muslim and/or Middle East villain
From Russia with Love (1963)	Raiders of the Lost Ark (1981)
White Nights (1985)	True Lies (1994)
Rocky IV (1985)	Executive Decision (1996)
Russkies (1987)	East is East (1998)
Die Hard (1988)	The Siege (1998)
Hunt for Red October (1990)	Rules of Engagement (2000)

- In what light are the antagonists portrayed?
- What physical descriptors are used to identify a certain group or individual?
- What emotional attributes are given to the antagonist?
- Are the antagonistic characters developed as flat (two-dimensional) characters, or do they have a complex, rounded character development?

Now contrast the antagonist to the protagonist:
- What physical and emotional traits identify the protagonist?
- What symbolic identifiers are used to create the protagonist's identity?
- In what ways does the story create a sense of emotional attachment to the protagonist (if any)?

Given the dualism between the protagonist and antagonist, consider the following:
- Can you think of examples of movies that counter these single narratives and false dichotomies?
- In what ways do you think that these movies influence the way a public perceives a group of individuals?

The construction of knowledge in the classroom

It is inconceivable to think that schools can be immune to such influences in the construction of knowledge for children. What counts as knowledge? How is knowledge represented and presented? Who decides the extent to which knowledge is constructed in the classroom? How is knowledge understood and assessed? Schools are inherently value-laden (McLaughlin, 1994). For example, schools in England and the United States, for the most part, do not conduct classes during the weekend. We tend to have winter breaks and spring breaks that coincide with Christian holidays. And while the terminology has changed to represent the secular nature, the correlation to Christian holidays is notable.

If the scheduling of schooling is considered value-laden, inside the school walls proves even more contentious. 'Schools and teachers exist for particular purposes, all of which assume the value of what is being aimed at' (*ibid.*, p. 454). Even if teachers attempt to create a neutral space in which to deliberate ideas – a safe haven one might say – how material is introduced and presented and what is omitted all have explicit and implicit value judgements.

Take, for instance, a number of children's picture books that were published to help children come to terms with the events of 9/11. The following authors have developed a number of stories targeting different age levels to assist teachers and adults in initiating an otherwise difficult talk about terrorism. Many consider *On that Day: A Book of Hope for Children* (2002) to be one of the 'canonical' storybooks for younger audiences in dealing with the events of 9/11. The syntax is simple and rhythmic following a common textual pattern used in children's books. It begins:

The world is blue
The word is green ...
The world is very big, and really round, and pretty peaceful.
(Patel, 2001)

The depiction is one of serenity and calm, where children are happy and do not feel scared or find themselves in difficult living circumstances. In addressing the events, the book continues: 'One day a terrible thing happened. The world ... got badly hurt. Many people were injured. Many other people died. And everyone was sad.' In trying to gain a sense of control in children's lives, the reader is told to share, play and laugh. The moral is one of hope and agency. No actual details of the event are brought forth, but lie in odd silence. The book places the burden on restoring justice and order on the child through the whimsical play and virtues, and hopes that their naive optimism will overcome the horrors of terrorism. As Connolly aptly points out,

> *On that Day* moves the personal to a vastly political scale (or conversely, the political to a vastly personal scale) at the same time that it ignores political context and positions the young

reader as a symbol of redemptive innocence and an outland-
ishly powerful Romantic Child who can repair the world and
ultimately end terrorism.

(2008, pp. 290–1)

The redemptive nature of such books may provide reassurance to
children, but it does little in addressing the events in any direct way.
While they may provide a heart-warming story, the abstract nature
surrounding the events may obfuscate and confuse the child, and
may not actually set out the task that it was intended to do. The
burden rests with the teacher or adult figure to develop or continue
the conversation should they so wish.

Another tactic commonly used in children's books focuses on
the heroism found on that day. In *Fireboat: The Heroic Adventures
of the John J. Harvey* (Kalman, 2002), the story situates itself with
the rise and prominence of New York with its iconic buildings
and places. A fireboat is launched in 1931 that parallels major
milestones of New York's power and stability, including how:
'"The Empire State building went up, up, up", Babe Ruth made his
611th home run, and George Washington Bridge was completed'
(cited in Connelly, 2008, p. 294). Now, 70 years later, the fireboat
is being considered too old to serve its purpose in relation to the
newer and faster fireboats in New York. Then in a stark turn of the
page, the pages turn from colour to grey, and over two pages the
author addresses the events of September 11:

> But then on September 11, 2001
> Something so huge and horrible
> Happened that the whole world
> Shook.
> It was 8:45 am in the morning,
> Another beautiful and sunny day.

Then when you turn the page you read:

> Two airplanes
>   Crashed into the Twin Towers
>   CRASHED, CRASHED, CRASHED into these
> two strong buildings.

(Kalman, 2002)

Here, the author has not shied away from the actual events of the story. The page depicts two airplanes, one placed slightly ahead of the other to connote the subtle difference between the first and the second planes' approaching impact on the World Trade Center. The Twin Towers loom ominously on the right side of the double page awaiting the impending disaster. In what proceeds, however, is the heroism that the *John J. Harvey* fireboat takes in playing a role in the rescue efforts to quench the fires of the Twin Towers. The parallel of the fireboat is that of a child, once considered 'small and powerless', but still able to assist and play a contributing role in both the short and long-term efforts to rebuild New York (*ibid.*, pp. 296–7).

While the *John J. Harvey* is a symbolic representation of a small child, the story *The Chapel that Stood* (Curtiss, 2003) tells of the heroism and self-sacrifice of firefighters coming to the aid of the victims inside the Twin Towers. Again, starting with the historical presence and stability of the building of the St Paul Chapel in 1776, tying that date to the period of George Washington and their family worshipping at the chapel and the grave of Alexander Hamilton nearby, it provides a historical foundation and prominence that the chapel is symbolic of standing the test of time amid tragic events. Again, set in a rhythmic textual pattern, the events unfold:

Two planes hi-jacked by a terrorist crew
Struck the Twin Towers: no warning, no clue!
Who thought it could happen, or knew what to do?
Fireman came and New York's Men in Blue.

… Firemen hung their shoes on the fence and raced to help the people in the towers:

Oh what gallant men did we lose
Who never came back to get their shoes.

(Curtiss, 2003)

The image of the shoes is a powerful way of showing those lives lost in attempts to save others from the burning towers. In the final pages of the book, the reader is again moved by the resilience, bravery and solidarity of the people of New York. The final call is of action in combating terrorism. In order to stop terrorism, everyone has a part to play like a 'link on a chain'. The ending is of solidarity and their patriotic stance toward America and that of freedom.

Before we move on to school textbooks, let us contrast and sum up *On That Day, Fireboat* and *The Little Chapel that Stood.* We find the events of September 11 primarily focus on the Twin Towers with little reference to Flight 93 (with the exception of the *Little Chapel that Stood,* which makes direct reference to it as an aside). *On that Day* relies on an adult who is reading the story to the child to provide the actual details of the event and initiate the conversation. Without this additional debate, children would not be provided with the facts regarding the unfolding of the events of September 11, as much of the content refers to the events in an abstract way. *Fireboat* and *The Little Chapel that Stood* focus on the unwavering strength of the United States prior to and post-September 11. Acts of heroism engage the reader with the details of the event told around these stories. Common morals in all three stories are based on the principle that children can make a difference to the world by playing their part to end terrorism and to make the world a better place. The 'soft option' technique of providing young children with a sense of agency is characterized by protraction and protection (Brocklehurst, 2006 and 2011).

Older children's literature takes on a more explicit and graphic element in depicting September 11. In children's literature aimed at ages 9 and up, common images of the impact of the Twin Towers may be shown either on the cover of the book or within the body of the text. Pictures of rubble and dust are also prevalent. Rarely does a book go by without the picture of the firemen raising the American flag being used, signifying both the courage and tireless efforts of the firemen and the patriotic stance of America. Yet, a titillating element occurs in some of the books whereby the intent is to engage and 'hook' the child to read about the accounts. In the book *Attack on America: The day the Twin Towers Collapsed* (Gow, 2002) the image of the Twin Towers on fire is displayed on the cover page. Graphic personal accounts are recollected by survivors and eyewitness accounts of the descriptive nature of the event, including specific references to skin being burnt or hanging off of a person, body parts found in the streets, people being thrown through walls or blown out of the building. The intent is to cement a graphic mental image in the child, particularly those who may not recall the actual event. Little is provided in the concluding chapter 'Why?' other than a rhetorical stance that understanding the terrorists' motives will do little to ease the trauma that America has faced.

The plethora of children's books on 9/11 is increasing (and interestingly, fewer such books are evident on 7/7 in the UK). Broadly speaking they work around common themes of courage, self-sacrifice, patriotism, heroism and hope. In the higher level reading series, a graphic, militaristic element appears in the violent, graphic images and textual recollections from eyewitnesses and survivors. In those cases, a sense of vigilance becomes apparent in the need to be on alert and to protect one's fundamental freedoms. The books offer a way to introduce the child to the events, but it is far from clear about how best to approach the topic.

School textbooks exhibit a similar lack of continuity and consensus about how to address the issue. Given the industry around publication and distribution of textbooks (which I alluded to in the previous chapter), along with a wide range of perspectives on how one might broach the topic, teachers receive little clear direction or guidance on how best to do so. Diana Hess and Jeremy Stoddard have done an extensive analysis of American textbooks to see how 9/11 was being presented and addressed (Hess and Stoddard, 2007; Hess, 2009). They note a number of interesting findings from their search of publications. In the first instance, most textbooks addressed the issue of 9/11, and warranted time and space to be given to be discussed in the classroom. Yet in many of the publications little detail was provided on the actual events of the day, and basic content was commonly absent from the texts. Whereas details about the Pearl Harbor attacks of 1941 would state how many people were killed and the intent behind the attacks, such information was not present in the 9/11 attacks. This is noteworthy, as Hess and Stoddard (2006) outline, as many of the children would have been very young or not yet born by the time they reached secondary schooling.

Common words and phrases were often used to describe the event. Without exception, all comment that the attack was an act of terrorism, and commonly, words such as 'horrific', 'tragic', 'evil', 'horrendous plot' and 'unprecedented' described the event (*ibid.*, p. 232). Most American textbooks also came from the perspective that this event was a turning point in history, not only in America, but for the world. The gravity of the event is taken to international levels.

Pictures were commonly used in the textbooks, again similar to the children's literature, often with the aftermath of the event, with firemen with dust on their face, firemen looking at the rubble, the American flag being raised at Ground Zero. And throughout, the themes of 'patriotism, nationalism and heroism' are the clear emphasis in the publications (*ibid.*, p. 233). Little critical analysis is provided regarding the nature of terrorism, or the contested notion of terrorism. Further, little critique is provided to questioning whether America may have been complicit in its foreign policy in the lead up to 9/11. Hess and Stoddard (2006) found the complete opposite stance: 'The United States is presented as a victim that deserved and received the world's support in the wake of 9/11' (p. 235).

The construction of knowledge in both children's literature and school textbooks echoes the messages found in the larger public sphere. It creates simple, single narratives that reinforce a mythology around the events. Acts of bravery are told in place of the miscommunication between the emergency services. Children are seen as the beacon of hope and innocence through their child-like behaviours that will help to overcome terrorism. Textbooks fall back on hero worship and provide a soft option for those who wish not to discuss the difficult or complex aspects of the events. In effect, a whitewashing of history occurs in our sanitizing of the events and the emphasis and de-emphasis of certain facts and circumstances surrounding an event (Leahey, 2010).

Pause for thought

I have highlighted a number of ways in which the events of 9/11 have been represented in children's literature and some of the common overlapping themes found in American textbooks. Reflect on the various examples that I have highlighted above, and consider how knowledge is constructed.

- Certain themes are emphasized in the representation of the events, including patriotism, heroism, courage and sacrifice. Can you think of any other themes that should be included in these texts?
- Connelly (2008) argues that children's books that provide a 'soft option' in addressing 9/11 may fail to address the

needs of children who are struggling to understand and cope. Do you agree or disagree?

- What images should be used in depicting 9/11?
- What are the purposes of these textbooks in presenting information? Is the purpose to provide descriptive material? To provide emotional support? To understand the political processes? To engage in debate? To critically reflect? To understand the historical event? To develop certain virtues and dispositions in oneself?

Conclusion

The way in which information is presented in various media comes with certain biases and perspectives. The way in which I write this book will have a particular stance, even in my best attempts to present a balanced view of how terrorism is considered in educational contexts. Yet, the ways in which the events are portrayed, particularly related to 9/11, create a 'moral rhetoric of evil and justice and encouraged to cultivate a sense that we are engaged in a battle of good and evil' (Govier, 2002, vii). Even if well intentioned, as in the case of many of the children's literature, the debates become polarized and oversimplified so that circumstances leading up to the event and the ways in which we attend to it in its aftermath are distorted. The potential extremist rhetoric further exacerbates tensions and creates false dichotomies. The events are simply brushed off that it was the work of extremist religious fanatics, rather than considering the rise in such movements that lead such individuals to commit such crimes. Further, building upon our fear and resentment of those of non-Western values creates a further chasm and has the potential to create a vicious cycle of long-standing hatred and resentment between groups of individuals.

It is clear that textbooks have explicit values that are expressed and brought forth in addressing these terrorist events. In the next chapter, I wish to consider how a teacher creates a space for addressing such controversial and sensitive topics. What is clear is that it is not just what is presented, but how it is presented and approached that ultimately influences and informs children's judgements about particular issues.

Further reading

Much has been written on the construction of knowledge and the way in which language has been used to depict terrorist events and the individuals implicated. For thorough elaboration about the way in which language has been used in the public media, read *War of Words: Language, politics and 9/11* (Silbertstein, 2002) and *(Mis) Representing Islam: The racism and rhetoric of British Broadsheet newspapers* (Richardson, 2004).

For a critique in the way knowledge is constructed between dualism of 'Western' and 'non-Western' thought, I recommend that you read *Identity and Violence: The Illusion of Destiny* (Sen, 2006) and *Power and Terror: Post-9/11 talk and interviews* (Chomsky, 2003).

Much attention has been given to the way in which the publishing industry related specifically to social studies textbooks has created certain perspectives and conversely has had omissions in the teaching of particular political and historic events. *Whitewashing War: Historical myth, corporate textbooks, and possibilities for democratic education* (Leahey, 2010) and *Teaching What Really Happened: How to avoid the tyranny of textbooks and get students excited about doing history* (Loewen, 2010) both provide a nuanced examination into the industry and the decisions about how social studies curricula are constrained and controlled.

For specific attention related to the emphases given to the events of 9/11, Diana Hess offers a succinct chapter on 9/11 in her book, *Controversy in the Classroom: The democratic power of discussion* (Hess, 2009).

Finally, you may wish to read some of the key titles in children's literature to see the visual imagery used to complement the text and the themes used to depict 9/11:

- *On that Day: A Book of Hope for Children* (Patel, 2002)
- *Fireboat: The Heroic Adventures of the John J. Harvey* (Kalman, 2002)
- *The Chapel that Stood* (Curtiss, 2003).

CHAPTER FOUR

Controversy at the School Gates

It is clear that the issue of extremism and terrorism harbours many emotive responses. Schools are often called to address controversial issues within the curricula that are contested among the public (How did dinosaurs become extinct? Should sexual education be a compulsory subject in schools?). Other topics may be sensitive, but not necessarily controversial. We may find the topic of death or divorce a difficult topic for children to address given the emotional gravitas that it has on their personal lives. The topic of extremism and terrorism, however, are both sensitive and controversial in nature. 'A topic qualifies as a sensitive controversy when it is both a matter of public dispute or contention and an issue on which people are easily moved to distress, anger or offence' (Hand et al., 2010). Sensitive controversies can be made harder for schools to handle by heated public debate about how they should do so.

One might argue that the issues of terrorism and extremism are not a sensitive controversy. Surely they are sensitive in that they are difficult to talk about, but they may not be controversial in the sense that they are simply morally wrong. No debate exists that the acts of terrorism warrant serious consideration, at least in an educational setting. In this sense, a moral directive is both appropriate and necessary to inculcate in children as part of their own moral development. Yet, even in some of the classrooms we debate this very notion when we consider questions such as 'Is there a difference between a terrorist and a freedom fighter?', 'Can state-sanctioned violent acts on civilians be considered acts of terrorism?' and so forth. Does it make a difference whether long-standing oppression or war-torn strife has made individuals undertake acts of violence on civilians. One need not look far to consider the acts in the Irish Republican Army (IRA) to at least acknowledge that the justifications behind the IRAs attacks hold resonance for a number of people in their long-standing strife with the English. What we may find is that the rationale behind the terrorist acts is compelling, but the actual terrorist acts morally wrong. We will return to this issue later in this chapter.

Given that terrorism and extremism are clearly sensitive in nature and difficult to address, and arguably are controversial in that opposing views are apparent in the justifications for terrorism, at least three important normative questions need to be asked about the teaching of sensitive controversies in schools:

1. Should sensitive controversies be tackled by schools at all?
2. If so, how should they tackle them?
3. When, if ever, should schools promote a particular view on a sensitive controversial issue?

As such, the overarching aim of this chapter is to consider how teachers might broach the topic in highlighting the moral and practical implications of addressing sensitive controversies in the classroom, particularly relating to the issue of extremism and terrorism.

Should terrorism or extremism be addressed at all?

The teaching of extremism and terrorism is incredibly difficult to navigate, with severe potential repercussions in terms of criticism from the public and parents, and a teacher's potential dismissal in the ways in which the topic is addressed. Three reasons might be given for not teaching sensitive controversies in the classroom:

1. Schools should not have to shoulder the burden of society's troubles.

2. Little consensus exists for how a teacher should broach the topic.

3. Little professional development or training may be given to teachers in how they should approach the topic appropriately.

Let us consider each of these justifications in turn.

A common concern and complaint among educators is that schools are increasingly asked to address issues that appear to be unresolved or contentious in the broader public sphere. The basis for England's 1944 Education Act called for one compulsory subject – that of religion – to restore the need for moral and character dispositions following the destruction of the Second World War. A decrease in voter participation in the democratic processes often elicits a call for increased citizenship and social studies curricula. If a perception exists that children are becoming increasingly rude and belligerent, calls for character education arise. Increased teenage pregnancy and sexually transmitted infections (STIs) create further debate on human sexuality subjects. It is unsurprising, then, that when a sensitive controversy arises regarding 9/11 and 7/7 calls for schools to help students both cope emotionally and cognitively understand the events are placed on the schools themselves. As Bernstein (1970) aptly put, 'schools cannot compensate for society' (p. 344). Schools are one of many public institutions that must bear the responsibility for developing our youth.

Consider the recent demands placed on schools. Schools are called upon to raise achievement levels in students' literacy and numeracy. Increasingly, we require students to develop critical capacities and reflection and to be engaged and for entrepreneurial thinkers to meet the demands of the twenty-first century. We criticize schools for not teaching enough history and science, yet add new demands for addressing obesity through more physical education and health classes, and develop their sense of creativity through arts and humanities classes. And we ask schools to do this within the confines of the six-hour day, reduced budgets and changing demographics of families and students. Surely, this is a tall order to fill? And if we ask teachers and schools to meet all of these demands, we expect that they will do it *well*, normally with little extra financial provision to ensure its success.

Given the numerous expectations, often pulling in different directions, one might suggest that the issue of terrorism and extremism is so contentious and sensitive that perhaps schools do not need to add this to their never-ending to-do list. One might suggest that simply teaching the social studies or citizenship curriculum in its broadest sense may be sufficient. We might, for instance, argue that what is required is not specific reference to the events of 9/11 or 7/7, but a broader understanding of the historical, political and social movements that shape and change our societies. We may also suggest that the events of 9/11 and 7/7 could detract from the significance of the political and social contexts surrounding such an event, and instead focus on the sensational, graphic moments of those particular days. In this sense, teaching about terrorism and extremism within the context of 9/11 and 7/7 does a disservice to understanding the arguably greater underpinning themes and issues that arise.

Pause for thought

Consider the arguments above, and reflect on how persuasive the arguments NOT to teach extremism and terrorism are.

- Do schools shoulder the burden of society? Is this appropriate?
- What should be the main priorities for schools to teach?
- If you could develop a list of the top ten things a teacher ought to teach in schools, what would that be? What did you leave out and why?

If you remain unconvinced by this line of reasoning, you would not be alone in this regard. And if your starting premise is that 9/11 was a turning point in world history (as many American books state), then the justifications to remove such discussions from within the school walls are not compelling. The way in which language changes, enemies are formed and changes in local and foreign policy evolve as a result of such events may require an understanding of those events. The challenge for teachers becomes 'Now what?'

I will not go to great lengths about the lack of consensus of how one should broach the topic of terrorism and extremism as this has already been done. It does highlight the problematic nature of how teachers must negotiate the multiple and contested ways in which one should teach about 9/11 and 7/7. What emphases should be given to the topic? How much detail is required or sufficient for children to understand about the events? Should a teacher develop lesson plans around certain values – toleration, respect, patriotism, courage, heroism, solidarity – or focus on the political and religious complexities prior to and following the events? How much time should be given to the topic? And at what ages should this topic be addressed? Should it be recurring and developmental over a number of years, or should it be discussed in depth at one particular moment during one's schooling? Such decisions are left largely up to the teacher within the broader parameters of curricular objectives and state or national guidelines. What we are largely left with is an inconsistent and patchy approach to addressing such issues. And unlike a traditional subject like mathematics, where there is a clarity and progression of thought and development, such is not the case with terrorism and extremism.

One might pause and consider whether professional development or teacher training programmes offer any guidance on the topic of terrorism and extremism. And again, the same inconsistency appears to exist largely dependent on the institution, the parameters of the teacher training programmes and the willingness of the lecturer or instructor. With few exceptions, teacher training programmes provide little explicit guidance on how to address terrorism and extremism. The focus tends to be broader, considering whether teachers should facilitate controversial discussions and the concomitant ethical and legal issues inherent in taking up such discussions. At other times, the topic might be addressed in peace education or international education within educational studies, but again such courses tend to be offered at a graduate level rather than within the parameters of undergraduate programmes. Curriculum studies (such as character education, citizenship and social studies) may address the issue, but commonly peripherally as one of many controversial topics that may be addressed in the class.

Given the large void in the preparation of teachers to address the issues of terrorism and extremism, other not-for-profit organizations attempt to offer professional development courses. The Facing History and Ourselves organization is an international educational and professional development organization whose mandate is to:

> … engage students of diverse backgrounds in an examination of racism, prejudice and anti-Semitism in order to promote the development of a more humane and informed citizenry.
>
> (Facing History, 2011)

Located in major cities throughout the United States and increasing partnerships in Northern Ireland, England, Belgium, Rwanda and Israel, it provides services and instructional guides for teachers and administrators to address sensitive controversies under the larger mandate of combating injustices and prejudices among individuals and nations. This particular non-profit organization is but one of the few exceptions that promote professional development offered to teachers. Most of the advice and guidance comes from the plethora of internet searches that range in quality and appropriateness with little critical review.

Pause for thought

At this point, one might feel dejected or overwhelmed by the obstacles in place with regard to teaching terrorism and extremism. Consider your own particular experiences:

- To what extent does your local educational authority or district provide a policy or professional development in addressing the issues of terrorism and extremism?
- If it is not explicitly stated anywhere, is the topic covered in another subject area indirectly (i.e. through English literature, counselling, health education)?
- What provisions have been provided within your own previous educational training or professional development workshops? Have they proved useful?
- If you are currently a teacher, what resources or references have you used to teach about terrorism and extremism? Were they recommended by your local educational authority, or did you find them on your own?

- What collaborative opportunities have you had in discussing how teachers might address the topic of terrorism and extremism? Has the school adopted any principles or guidelines in how one might address the topic? Or is it left up to the discretion of the teacher?

How to broach terrorism and extremism in the classroom

If you have read this far, and have not been persuaded that schools should not enter into this debate, it follows that teachers now have to negotiate this difficult tightrope of how to address terrorism and extremism in schools. One might suggest that the actual topic of terrorism and extremism has been discussed to some extent prior to the events of 9/11 and 7/7, and rightly so. Yet these recent attacks (and on American soil, a relatively unscathed part of the world relative to other countries – i.e. Israel or Palestine – that have longstanding periods of violence) make the topic that much more sensitive and emotionally trying than other events.

Given this contentious topic, one might suggest that a teacher should remain neutral and provide a safe haven for open facilitation to the extent that is possible. Letting students come to understand and reconcile their feelings and understandings of an event may provide greater awareness of the issues at hand. Hess et al. (2008) considered the extent to which the disclosure of teachers' opinions affected students and the implications of teachers' disclosure to that of their own alignment of the views of the teacher. In the data collected, teachers sat along a continuum regarding the extent to which they should disclose their own views. At one end of the spectrum, teachers thought that in order to create a safe environment where students could explore their understandings and views on a particular issue, it was critical that teachers remain neutral and not express their own viewpoints. At the other end of the spectrum, teachers think that it is facile to attempt to stay neutral on a topic, and have instead taken the view that one should disclose on a particular issue. And for the most part, teachers struggled with issues of disclosure generally, particularly if they were 'so heavily invested emotionally, intellectually into these issues' (Hess, 2009, p. 100).

The concern with disclosure is not in sharing a particular view, but the power of authority and influence that a teacher has on the development of students' understandings and perceptions about the world. The nature of the sensitive controversial issue is such that any set of reasonable opposing views towards an issue must then require teachers not to put forth a particular stance for fear of being biased. Taking an ideological stance, particularly when the issue is far from uncontested or heated, may prove not only controversial among the teaching profession but may be a legal liability and may be cause for dismissal (Associated Press, 2007).

And unlike other venues where debates and views are expressed, children are compelled to attend school and in that sense are part of a captive audience of a particular authority figure – who not only provides and presents knowledge and values, but also assesses students. The fear is that students may align their views with that of their teachers with little critical reflection or understanding, but simply to gain favour and sympathy by the teacher.

Three compelling issues arise in this debate about whether to disclose or not. First, students want the opportunity to discuss and deliberate on a particular issue on their own at first. By letting them work it out for themselves, they are not just going through the pros and cons of a particular debate, but are consciously working through the merits of the debates and trying to come to terms of the issue on their own (Hess, 2009, pp. 107–8). Coupled with this view, however, is the fact that students wish to be liked and respected by the teacher. Students hope that the teacher will appreciate their views and feel a sense of worth in developing their position; conversely, students fear the repercussions from expressing an opposing view. Finally, students wish to conduct a debate within the principles of respect during deliberative discussions. A notion of allowing students to feel safe in sharing their opinions without fear of reprisal is of paramount importance.

Similar to these issues, Hess (2009) suggests that in allowing teachers to disclose their views a number of unintended consequences may arise. If teachers provide their perspective first, students may simply talk less. Being handed a perspective by the teacher does not allow for children to construct their own knowledge. It is a top-down perspective that makes students passive in their learning. Second, students thought that the tone of the classroom might change if the perspective of the teacher was known. Hess does note, however, that this concern was only noted by students who attended classes where teachers did not disclose their views (2009, p. 108). Finally, students felt that they would need to 'work harder to understand the issues when they do not know the teacher's opinions' (*ibid*., p. 108). The onus and responsibility in a classroom where the teacher does not disclose rests with the student.

When we delve into moral issues, particularly in developing children's dispositions to learn right from wrong, good from bad, morally righteous from morally abhorrent, we enter a debate about the extent to which schools should put forth certain moral claims. We further may have a spectrum of permissibility that teachers can make regarding certain moral claims, from thin or abstract principles to thick assertions about what constitutes a good life. We come to a crossroads regarding how teachers might approach moral decisions. One might take a *directive* approach 'when it is undertaken with the aim of imparting moral beliefs, when there is a deliberate attempt to persuade children of the truth or correctness of moral claims' (Hand, 2009, p. 1). Conversely, a *non-directive* approach might be appropriate 'when discussion of moral beliefs is open-ended, when children are encouraged to interrogate and assess moral claims but brought under no pedagogical pressure to accept or reject them' (*ibid*., p. 1).

But surely this cannot always be the case when controversial issues arise. Hand (2007) points this out when we consider the guidelines on 'racist bullying' offered by TeacherNet, an online resource in the United Kingdom. It states that teachers provide, '"a balanced presentation of opposing views" when bringing controversial issues to students' attention, which in practice means "giving equal importance to conflicting views and opinions" and "presenting all information and opinion as open to interpretation, qualification and contradiction"' (TeacherNet, cited in Hand, 2008, p. 216). Hand rightly points out that certain controversial issues ought to have a moral directive by teachers. It is not simply about providing a fair and balanced perspective – there is an explicit moral imperative that we should direct the students in a particular moral and ethical direction. One could conjecture that if students were simply left to their own devices to negotiate the events of 9/11 or 7/7 with little direction from the teacher in the spirit of open-facilitation and neutrality, they might come to the conclusion that they should have a deep-seated fear and hatred of all Muslims. And given the public and media portrayal of anti-Muslim sentiment in the newspapers, on the television and in popular culture, this would not be too far-fetched to imagine. It is clear that this would be an inappropriate stance for children to take given that the vast majority of Muslims are moderate and live peacefully and cohesively in mainstream British and American societies. Simply providing open facilitation may not be enough from the teacher in this case.

We come to the next quandary in this debate. On the one hand, students feel as though they take ownership and responsibility of their learning, and hope to have a fairer playing field if teachers do not disclose their personal views (Hess, 2009). On the other hand, some sensitive controversies require not just mere open facilitation, but some moral directive to guide students (Hand, 2006, 2008, 2010). One can easily become stuck in some philosophical moral quagmire. While philosophers may pontificate and debate the merits and demerits of how best to approach the issue of values, schools simply have to move on in the daily lives of teaching students. As is evident, values do not live in a vacuous, abstract space, but play out in the events and lives of particular issues and events; 'they require practical interpretation and application' (McLaughlin, 1994, p. 473). It is a logistical problem as well because we cannot simply 'stop the clock' until we come to consensus:

> Schools do not enjoy the luxury of being able to engage in extended clarificatory debate. Policies about present and future practice must be formulated and acted upon, and cannot wait for agreed conclusions from philosophical discussions ... the demands of clarity must be kept in balance with the other demands of educational planning and management ... [and] bringing into sharp focus the full extent of disagreement between teachers can result in the inhibition of practical consensus and effective action. Ambiguity has a constructive and lubricative role here.
>
> (*ibid.*, pp. 476–7)

Attempting absolute certainty and clarity is largely unachievable when we consider terrorism and extremism, and it seems similarly unhelpful for teachers simply to avoid the topic as a result of its ambiguity and difficulty.

If we take a *directive* approach to those controversial issues, where compelling rational reasons exist for persuading children towards a particular stance, what moral standards do we use? This question thus takes us to the final part of the chapter in debating which values should be put forth when we consider terrorism and extremism. Before moving on to this final question, let us pause again to consider the points made in this section.

Pause for thought

- What role should teachers play in addressing sensitive controversies such as terrorism and extremism?
- Should a teacher disclose their opinions or remain neutral?
- Is the matter of teacher disclosure dependent on the nature of the topic? Would it make a difference whether we were talking about another issue related to politics, history, English or science? Would it matter whether the event occurred in the past (such as Pearl Harbor) or had been in recent living memory? Should that make a difference?
- Where do you stand regarding *directive* and *non-directive* approaches to issues that have significant moral and value judgements? Should the classroom discussion be through open facilitation and exploration by the students, or is there a moral imperative that ought to be directed by the teacher?

We are getting to the crux of how one might approach the issues of terrorism and extremism in schools, particularly when moral beliefs and value judgements are inherently embedded in the nature of the topic.

When, if ever, should schools promote a particular view on a sensitive controversial issue?

Much debate has arisen regarding moral education and the extent to which teachers should put forth a particular moral directive. Disagreements abound regarding what constitutes the 'common good', values to which everyone can ascribe, particularly when we have fundamentally different philosophical, political or religious views about what the good life entails. The intent is that by having a common shared identity, this in turn would help foster a more cohesive and stable society. Shared norms and values helps to create this level of cohesiveness. Michael Walzer (1983) for instance, suggests:

> Every substantive account of justice is a local account ... One characteristic above all is central to my argument. We are (all of us) culture-producing creatures; we make and inhabit meaningful worlds. Since there is no way to rank and order these worlds with respect to their understanding of social goods, we do justice to men and women by respecting their particular creations ... Justice is rooted in the distinct understandings of places, honors, jobs, things of all sorts that constitute a shared way of life. To override those understandings is (always) to act unjustly.
>
> (Walzer, 1983, p. 314)

What is central to Walzer's argument is that shared cultural under-standings rest with the political community. We understand our fellow citizens through the meanings that we share – without that we cannot come to agreement about the principles that provide the foundation for a political structure.

The common criticism of Walzer's claim is that the suggestion that there is a particular common good assumes a too homogenous picture of society. It silences or represses those on the fringes, be it women, ethnic minorities or children. It paints a picture of a culture that is somewhat ossified – a political culture that is rarely if ever to be challenged, but assumed as part of the status quo. The notion of a common shared identity is one that is rightly challenged by feminists who wish to challenge the dominant discourse of a particular society (Moller-Okin, 1999; Young, 2000; Nussbaum, 2003). Others assert that creating such a 'community' conceals and represses discourses of power (Rose, 1999; Fendler, 2001).

Yet, Walzer's argument for a shared political culture does resonate to some degree. It seems reasonable to suggest that a minimum level of shared values is required in order that people contribute to and abide by the political rules and regulations that govern a society. Joseph Carens (2000) supports Walzer and suggests that the notion of a common good does not necessarily require that the 'common good' is all-encompassing. One can have a shared political culture without it assuming all of one's culture. So long as we acknowledge: '(1) some range of morally permissible implementations on any given account of the principles and (2) some range of reasonable disagreement about how to interpret the principles themselves' we can have some sympathy for Walzer's arguments (Carens, 2000, p. 28). A minimum threshold of a common political structure seems valid in pursuing and protecting.

The basis for such a shared common political criterion is commonly found in Rawls' *Political Liberalism* (1993). Given the diverse demographics found in any society, individuals co-exist despite their competing and fundamental ideas about how to lead a fulfilling life (or among philosophical debates commonly articulated as 'competing conceptions of the good'). Simply put, individuals have different beliefs about how to lead their lives. Rawls states:

> The political culture of a democratic society is always marked by a diversity of opposing and irreconcilable religious, philosophical and moral doctrines. Some of these are perfectly reasonable, and this diversity among reasonable doctrines political liberalism sees as the inevitable long-run result of the powers of human reason at work within the background of enduring free institutions.
>
> (Rawls, 1993, pp. 3–4)

Given this premise, one might state that little moral directive can be provided when among a citizenry we have vastly multiple, and at times conflicting, values about how one should lead their life. And Rawls is reluctant to interfere in these multiple conceptions of the good for the most part. The state should, for the most part, not attend to those morals that address *comprehensive* doctrines about how to lead one's life. A comprehensive doctrine 'includes conceptions of what is of value in human life, and ideals of personal character, as well as ideals of friendship and of familiar associational relationships, and much else that is to inform our conduct, and in the limit to our life as a whole' (*ibid.*, p. 13). It is not the responsibility of public institutions (like the state) to interfere with one's private conceptions about what to believe and what to do in their private life.

Rawls advocates a political theory based on the central tenet of free and equal persons (*ibid.*, 3–4). By limiting liberal theory to a political conception, Rawls wishes to avoid the debating the merits and weaknesses of controversial religious, philosophical and moral doctrines, upon which it may be difficult for people to agree. In an increasingly pluralist society, it is difficult to achieve consensus based on a comprehensive moral doctrine. He states, 'I should like to avoid, for example, claims to universal truth, or claims about the essential nature and identity persons' (Rawls, 1985, p. 223). The principles of liberty and equality provide the basis for Rawls' political theory.

At this point, one might question to what extent this is of value if we are trying to bring forth some moral directives for terrorism and extremism. Hand (2010) contends that Rawls provides little assistance with giving educators any principles on how they might put forth a directive approach regarding moral education. He argues that if we agree with Rawls' point that reasonable pluralism requires not interfering with competing conceptions of the good, then it follows that it 'precludes the possibility of identifying a set of moral beliefs support by compelling reasons and therefore capable of being rationally imparted to children' (*ibid.*, p. 11). We either have to abandon the idea of a directive approach to moral education, or we have to abandon the idea of reasonable pluralism.

I think this is a limited interpretation of Rawls' reasonable pluralism and how it may be of assistance to teaching moral directives particularly related to terrorism and extremism. While the comprehensive moral doctrines should rightly be avoided given the founding principles that guide liberal democracies in protecting individuals' various fundamental freedoms (such as freedom of speech, association, religion, conscience and equality rights that protect individuals from discrimination based on age, gender, sexual orientation, race, etc.), one might use the *political* criterion for providing moral directives. A political conception is 'a moral conception worked out for a specific kind of subject, namely, for political, social and economic institutions' (Rawls, 1996, p. 11).

I suspect that some individuals will take issue with the statement that liberal democracies are built on the ideals of fundamental rights and freedoms, at least in practice. That said, we cannot simply deny that various Constitutions, charters and common law precedence aspire to these principles at the very least. I do not wish to belabour this point here as it is not the focus, but want to acknowledge that such a debate does exist in terms of the extent to which fundamental rights and freedoms are exercised in practice in Western democracies.

This does not mean that other virtues or dispositions are not helpful in strengthening and improving a society; rather other virtues, while important, fall subordinate to principles of justice:

> As citizens we have reasons to impose the constraints specified by the political principles of justice on associations; while as members of associations we have reasons for limiting those constraints so that they leave room for free and flourishing internal life appropriate to the association in question.
>
> (Rawls, 2001, p. 165)

An important value for people is to allow them to form, pursue and revise the way individuals choose to live their lives. Only when comprehensive doctrines infringe upon liberty and equality must they be constrained by justice. In this way, Rawls attempts to create a political theory based on reasonable pluralism.

The political criterion, however, has implicit moral directives embedded in the public political culture of a democratic society. He suggests that the public political culture is one that is based on a 'fair system of cooperation over time from one generation to the next' (*ibid.*. p. 5). The idea of social cooperation is a pivotal concept underpinning Rawls' theory:

(a) Social cooperation is distinct from merely socially coordinated activity – for example, activity coordinated by orders issued by an absolute central authority. Rather, social cooperation is guided by publicly recognized rules and procedures, which those cooperating accept as appropriate to regulate their conduct.

(b) The idea of cooperation includes the idea of fair terms of cooperation: these are terms each participant may reasonably accept, and sometimes should accept, provided that everyone else likewise accepts them. Fair terms of cooperation specify an idea of reciprocity, or mutuality: all who do their part as the recognized rules require are to benefit as specified by a public and agreed-upon standard.

(c) The idea of cooperation also includes the idea of participant's rational advantage, or good. The idea of rational advantage specified what it is that those engaged in cooperation are seeking to advance from the standpoint of their own good.

(Rawls, 1993, p. 6)

Firmly entrenched in this idea is the requirement that persons must have at least minimum levels of social interaction with others. Social cooperation entails that people will be rational and reasonable in coming together to determine a set of fair and just principles to regulate society. It requires individuals that will be acceptable to all.

The second aspect of Rawls' social cooperation addresses reciprocity and mutuality. The idea of reciprocity is that persons will be willing to accept certain principles that are agreed upon, even if they may not be to their personal advantage, so long as others do the same in order to maintain social justice in society. This differs from the notion of mutual advantage where individuals derive personal benefit from a particular situation. There appear to be at least two implicit components in the idea of reciprocity: one, an inherent trust that others will comply with the principles; and two, that by complying with the principles even if they may not affect me personally or may even be to some disadvantage, is nonetheless beneficial for a just and stable society. Social cooperation in this instance has a collective purpose attached to it: I will agree to and accept the principles knowing that it will be to the greater, public benefit of society, so long as others agree as well.

The last feature of Rawls' notion of social cooperation entails that it must be to each participant's rational advantage, or good. This is a protective assurance to ensure that participants are not constrained without their consent, nor are they being coerced into a practice they do not accept or are not comfortable with. Certain rules and procedures should not be to a person's detriment or against their will, nor should it suppress certain individuals for the advantage of others.

The question becomes whether political directives that have a clear moral stance be instructive when we teach terrorism and extremism. This line of reasoning is compelling in that it does not address a more contentious and invasive aspect of a directive moral approach that is comprehensive in nature. It attends to those public political dispositions that are hoped to provide the political stability and cohesiveness of the larger democratic sphere. Specifically, one might then focus on the moral directives inherent under the principles of justice and the central tenets underpinning free and equal persons.

Let us consider, however, that despite individuals' sincere attempts to 'draw inferences, weigh evidence, and balance competing considerations', we arrive at two completely reasonable yet differing and incompatible conclusions (Rawls 1993, p. 55). The consequence of using a fair system of social cooperation as the process for determining fair and just procedures is that there may still be disagreement among reasonable and rational persons. Rawls attends to this dilemma in what he refers to as 'the burdens of judgement'.

As reasonable and rational persons, we make different kinds of judgements in the deliberative process. Rawls provides a list, which is not exhaustive, that influences our judgements as reasonable and rational persons. Evidence may be complex and difficult to assess. Individuals may give different weight and import to various aspect of the issue, thus arriving at different conclusions. The subject matter for consideration, such as political or moral matters, may rely heavily on judgement and interpretation of how we assess and weigh the evidence and is shaped by our life experiences, which consequently may cause our judgements to diverge. Normative considerations and differing values on both sides of the debate make it difficult to have one answer or solution (*ibid.*, pp. 55–8). Rawls suggests that in circumstances where individuals have gone through this process, yet arrive at different conclusions, we have to foster toleration under the burdens of judgement within the boundaries of reasonable pluralism:

> The evident consequence of the burdens of judgement is that reasonable persons do not all affirm the same comprehensive

doctrine. Moreover, they also recognize that all persons alike, including themselves, are subject to those burdens, and so many reasonable comprehensive doctrines are affirmed, not all of which can be true (indeed none of them may be true). The doctrine any reasonable person affirms is but one reasonable doctrine among others.

(Rawls, 1993, p. 60)

What is considered to be reasonable, however, is broadly defined. Rawls has three criteria for determining reasonable doctrines. First, 'a reasonable doctrine is an exercise of theoretical reason: it covers the major religious, philosophical, and moral aspects of human life in a more or less consistent and coherent manner'. Second, 'a reasonable comprehensive doctrine is also an exercise of practical reason'. Third, 'while a reasonable comprehensive view is not necessarily fixed and unchanging, it normally belong to, or draws upon, a tradition of thought and doctrine' (*ibid.*, p. 59). Rawls does not want to evaluate comprehensive moral doctrines as to what is considered 'true' or 'correct'. If he is to be sincere about endorsing diversity and toleration, the political doctrine has to concede and allow unreasonable doctrines within the confines of reasonable pluralism.

That said, Rawls makes an important distinction for the allowance of *unreasonable* doctrines within the scope of reasonable pluralism that deserve our respect, from those of *intolerable* doctrines. We accept and assume that there will exist some forms of unreasonable doctrines. We tolerate those unreasonable doctrines in preserving the greater political ideals of diversity and toleration. Yet we constrain comprehensive doctrines that are intolerable: specifically, those that threaten and undermine the essential principles of justice that govern society.

How can we apply these broader political principles that have a clear moral directive for our purposes of addressing terrorism and extremism in the classroom? Let us pull out some of the clear moral implications and emphases that would then follow if we used the political criterion found within the concept of reasonable pluralism and the burdens of judgement. The first and central tenet is that of free and equal persons. If we are to talk about terrorism and extremism, the discussion is around fundamental rights and freedoms and the implications that such events have in compromising or changing those principles. It is fine, then, to talk about one's various issues of equality and freedom (assuming that it does not fall to the lowest common denominator of a debate between 'us' and 'them'). How can we protect and ensure that all citizens are treated as fair and equal persons?

Punishment of wrongdoing is appropriate under the conditions of justice. When the principles of justice have been compromised, one can condemn the actions and hold those individuals accountable for their crimes. Yet, within a Rawlsian framework, it must be done so that just institutions should be fair to all its members. Using a hypothetical thought process known as the veil of ignorance (Rawls, 1971), each individual is to consider how to develop just principles based on the idea that they do not know their own background. Each individual would not know their gender, their wealth, their racial or ethnic background, their political or religious beliefs. Using this thought process, it is hoped that individuals will develop the most reasoned and rational principles that would not favour any one particular individual or group to the disadvantage of others. Using the veil of ignorance then has a place in the penal system where the principles ought not to discriminate between one individual and the next. Not only one's own advantages or disadvantages would develop a just society that aims for impartiality and non-bias. And while this is an ideal abstract thought process, the intent is to mitigate from principles that target those individuals who may already be marginalized or discriminated against in mainstream society.

The second principle is that of social cooperation. How do individuals come together to deliberate and develop principles in how we need to live cohesively given the circumstances that surround such events? If we are to uphold the principle that we should refrain from interfering in one's comprehensive moral doctrines, one must teach the dispositions of toleration and respect under the larger political framework of reasonable pluralism. This would require us to break down the stereotypes of 'us' and 'them' and think in more nuanced ways of where we have some shared and overlapping values, even if some of those values may be viewed as unreasonable. We can temper those views that are considered *intolerable*, as Rawls rightly points out – those that threaten the stability of a political society – but those views are the exception and those that undermine the fundamental principles of justice.

Principles of justice, then, have a moral directive in the ways in which a teacher might approach the issue of terrorism and extremism. The focus becomes on ensuring the stability of public values and its implications for each individual's private comprehensive doctrines (so long as they are within the reasonable parameters set within the principles of justice). And similarly, when comprehensive doctrines do threaten the stability of society, teachers can condemn such actions and say that such acts are morally reprehensible. Teachers would then have a solid moral foundation in which to persuade students away from such intolerable doctrines. It would not simply be a case of allowing for those diverging opinions in a class. A moral directive to convince the student otherwise is both appropriate and necessary.

Pause for thought

This section has considered the extent to which teachers are able to provide a directive moral approach to the issues of terrorism and extremism. Consider the following:

- Do you agree with the concept of reasonable pluralism? Why or why not?
- Do you think that the principles of justice help teachers to put forth certain moral directives in their class?
- Are public values of justice sufficient to address terrorism and extremism in the class?

Conclusion

When we begin to break down what is at stake for teachers in addressing terrorism and extremism in the classroom, we see how they must negotiate a stream of difficult decisions that one must make with no clear answer. They may simply throw up their hands, and do little to address the topic given the emotive and sensitive nature of the subject matter. If they do decide to teach it, or are obliged to address it in their class, one may question whether they should remain neutral on the topic or provide a moral stance.

Students may find that working through the issues by themselves gives them the ownership and responsibility to work through them. And yet, one might suggest that the nature of the topic requires teachers to provide moral guidance and persuade students to see the act as morally wrong and abhorrent. Beyond that, one might consider whether there are private and public values that must be put forth by teachers.

Principles of justice may offer a way of providing a moral directive that ensures a political stability for society. Teachers and schools can also appropriately dissuade students from those private moral values that are intolerable and threaten the stability of society. In this way, we may find that the central tenets of free and equal persons together with the notion of social cooperation may help to frame the way in which a discussion about terrorism and extremism might occur in the classroom that fulfils the objectives of being informative and critically aware and the circumstances around the lead up to and aftermath of such events.

Let us now turn to the final chapter and pull all of the threads together in understanding and addressing terrorism and extremism in the classroom.

Further reading

Much debate has centred on the extent to which substantive issues can be raised in teaching citizenship. When such substantive issues as terrorism and extremism do arise, one must ask whether there is a moral directive inherent in such discussions. Terrance McLaughlin's article, 'Citizenship, Diversity and Education a philosophical perspective' (1994) has become a canonical text in considering thin and thick conceptions of citizenship.

Michael Hand has carried forward the work of Terrance McLaughlin in considering the extent to which sensitive controversies should be addressed in relation to homosexuality, bullying and patriotism. The application of the extent of moral directive in teaching sensitive controversies is played out in four key articles and has relevance for how educators consider how they would address terrorism and extremism in class. To see how this is applied in different contexts, I would recommend: 'Should we teach homosexuality as a controversial issue?' (Hand, 2007); 'What should we teach as controversial? A defense of the Epistemic Criterion' (Hand, 2008); and 'Patriotism in British Schools: Principles, practices and press hysteria' (Hand, 2009).

CHAPTER FIVE

Sensibility, Reasonableness and Moderation

We have come full circle regarding terrorism and extremism in the classroom. We touched on some of the multiple ways in which individuals, organizations and governments responded to the events of 9/11 and 7/11. Numerous other lessons plans, suggested activities, books and websites have attended to these issues that have not been noted here. One can do an independent search to find the multiple and contested ways in which extremism and terrorism have been presented. We have looked at some of the rationales used to address terrorism and extremism in the classroom, including: developing a more cohesive and stable society; understanding factors that may influence extremist activities; examining contemporary political affairs; developing dispositions that will make more individuals more tolerant, or conversely, make individuals more vigilant against terrorism. It is not hard to see the multiple ways in which terrorism and extremism are viewed and addressed when we take a step back and consider the way in which knowledge is constructed on the issues beyond the classroom walls. When we considered how teachers are to address the value and moral judgements inherent in such sensitive controversies, we looked at whether to disclose or remain neutral, keep the classroom open-ended or have a moral directive.

In this concluding chapter, I wish to consider four main recommendations for addressing terrorism and extremism in the classroom. This is not an exhaustive list, and although these are normative recommendations, it is the hope that such recommendations provide enough room for one's own professional judgement in addressing terrorism and extremism in the classroom that is educationally sound and critically attentive. And if by chance, at the end of this chapter, you vehemently disagree with these suggestions, I welcome you to enter this debate and put forth what you deem to be a more robust proposition.

As such, here are the central principles that ought to guide educators in the task of addressing terrorism and extremism.

1. Terrorism and extremism is a necessary and fundamental component that should be addressed in the curriculum.

2. Events such as 9/11 and 7/7 must be situated within the broader historical and political backdrop.

3. An examination of current inequitable circumstances that ostracize and marginalize certain groups to consider more extremist actions is required.

4. Open facilitation and neutrality is an insufficient stance for teachers and schools to take, and must be situated within a larger moral framework built on the political values necessary for a stable, civil society.

Principle one: terrorism and extremism should be addressed in the curriculum

It is clear that avoiding the topic of terrorism and extremism is a foolhardy approach to take, and can easily be ruled out. It affects the hearts and minds of those directly affected by terrorist acts, shapes the way in which we interact with individuals at a local level and, more importantly, influences national and international relations and foreign policies. Teachers cannot simply give it wide berth due to its sensitive and controversial nature, but have an obligation to equip students with the dispositions and critical capacity to negotiate such momentous historic events.

Whitewashing such conflict, as much of the local media did at the time, was noticeable by a number of students who critically examined one newspaper's coverage of the events. 'Many students were dismayed to find that their local media did not cover the social, political, and economic antecedents of the conflict, ignored international perspectives and voices of dissent, and focused on hawkish statements made by American military and political leaders (Leahey, 2010, p. 1). One of the few exceptions of books that provide a relatively objective historical account of 9/11 is that of *One Day in History: September 11, 2001* (Carlisle, 2007). Set up in almost an encyclopaedic format, Carlisle provides short, concise articles to much of the terminology and circumstances that surround 9/11. He begins with a chronology of the events that occurred on September 11, and thereafter provides articles in alphabetical order, key details, causes and consequences of that day. The objective of the book is that it is one of the few books that offer such basic information in which one can then move on to more critical reflection and reasoned judgement about September 11.

If we are serious about preparing our students for their ability to understand and exercise their rights in a democratic society, such dispositions cannot be left to chance. A political education requires that students be inducted into the larger political sphere:

> … it is a shared way of public life constituted by a constellation of attitudes, habits, and abilities that people acquire as they grow up. These include a lively interest in the question of what life is try and not just seemingly good, as well as a willingness both to share one's own answer with others and to heed the many opposing answers they might give; and active commitment to the good of the polity, as well as confidence and competence in judgment regarding how that good should be advanced; a respect for fellow citizens and a sense of common fate with them that goes beyond the tribalisms of ethnicity and religion and is yet alive to the significance these will have in many people's live.
>
> (Callan, 1997, p. 3)

Eamonn Callan calls forth a robust political education that does not shy away from such difficult subjects as terrorism and extremism that shape and inform the way in which individuals react and respond to such events. It is essential that children are active and engaged in the topics that will help them to form reasoned judgements, despite differing values and attitudes that are presented both in their private and public sphere. Simply shying away from the subject matter is a missed educational opportunity and a whitewashing of history.

Events that shape our history and our politics are integral to the way in which people live their lives; potentially removing these debates from classrooms minimizes the way in which individuals are able to address substantive pressing issues that are relevant in society. If educators are sincere about preparing students as future citizens, limiting discussion or removing potentially contentious issues that may cause offence or debate seems antithetical to fostering an active and engaged citizenry.

Principle two: 9/11 and 7/7 ought be taught within the broader historical and political backdrop

If the first principle is that an obligation exists that terrorism and extremism should be taught in the curriculum (and in particular the events of 9/11 and 7/7), the second principle recommends that it be situated in the larger historical and political landscape. At minimum, it would require schools to attend to the basic facts of such events. It is not adequate to assume that students will know the basic information about what occurred on those days.

That said, I can think of no reasonable justification for the need for lesson plans to focus on the titillating, graphic or sensationalist tone in depicting the events. Even if the public media chooses to emphasize such things in order to gain more viewers, that is not the role that schools ought to play. Human interest stories and survivors' harrowing escapes offer little educational import in developing one's critical capacities for reasoned reflection and judgement surrounding the attacks.

What is commonly agreed by those who specialize in counter terrorist or Middle East studies, is that one must come to understand the historical and political vestiges that lead up to such attacks. In Richardson's (2007) thorough explication of the rationale behind terrorist acts, what is clear is the robust historical and political accounts of various terrorist groups. In laying out the factors that give rise to more extremist activity, one begins to understand the justifications and rationales that lead individuals to undertake extreme acts. Richardson debunks many of the common myths about terrorism: that they are insane, immoral and evil. Yet, in laying out the complex political landscape, you begin to understand their actions. And while they are certainly not condonable, an awareness of the historical and political situations is central to understanding what drives individuals to extreme acts. When the claim is made that terrorists are 'insane', Richardson draws upon the numerous studies that have interviewed and studied the demographic of many terrorists. And in many of the cases, they are educated, middle-class, 'normal' individuals. The difference is that they view their political circumstances as dire and that they have no alternative but to turn to terrorism (*ibid.*, p. 16). Similarly, they may feel they have little other effective strategy to overthrow a regime. If membership is small and the regime has both financial and man power, then terrorist acts may be seen as the only effective way to change the political dynamics in which terrorists feel oppressed.

In a similar vein of understanding the historical and political terrain, one must come to understand differing cultures. Nothing is as unhelpful as lumping together a group of individuals from different religions, tribes, locations, ethnicities, races, etc. into a notion of the 'Other' (Sen, 2006). For instance, addressing the Islamic faith as if it was one large behemoth is particularly unhelpful and probably more harmful in creating further resistance and resentment.

> Other cultural generalizations, for example, about national, ethnic, or racial groups, can also resent astonishingly limited and bleak understandings of the characteristics of the human beings involved. When a hazy perception of culture is combined with fatalism about the dominating power of culture, we are, in effect, asked to be imaginary slaves of an illusory force ... Not only are the implicit and twisted beliefs frequently the subject matter of racist jokes and ethnic slurs, they sometimes surface as grand theories.
>
> (*ibid.*, pp. 103–4)

If the primary aim of teaching about the events of 9/11 and 7/7 is to gain clarity, develop critical reflection and make reasoned judgements, then a robust account of all that is involved is required.

Terrance McLaughlin (1992) articulates clear distinctions between minimum and maximum interpretations of what is required in developing citizenship in children. On a 'minimal' or 'thin' conception, citizenship is limited to the 'associated rights, within a community of a certain sort based on the rule of law ...' which may focus on things like 'the possession by a person of a passport, the right to vote and an unreflective "nationality"' (*ibid.*, p. 236). This last point, such as an unreflective position of one's nationality or patriotism, has had a clear emphasis in much of the textbooks and lesson plans surrounding the events of 9/11. Hand and Pearce (2009) suggest that while a love of one's country provides a certain emotional attachment, it is not necessarily the case that we should promote patriotism as an automatic good, particularly 'by means of rhetoric, ritual and propaganda' (p. 454). Despite the media outcry on their stance that patriotism should be taught as a neutral topic for open discussion among children, Hand and Pearce contend that such rhetoric and propaganda is 'precluded by the basic educational imperative to respect and to develop the rationality of our students' (*ibid.*, p. 455).

So if we go against the general tenor of much of the educational literature that focuses on this unreflective patriotism, then what might a maximum interpretation entail? Maximal views, in contrast, are:

> ... conceived in social, cultural and psychological terms. Thus, the citizen must have a consciousness of him or herself as a member of a living community with a shared democratic culture involving obligations and responsibilities as well as rights, a sense of the common good, fraternity and so on. This latter maximal, interpretation of the identity required by a citizen is dynamic rather than static in that it is seen as a matter for continuing debate and redefinition. It also gives rise to the question of the extent to which social disadvantage in its various forms can undermine citizenship, especially when a sense of effective personal agency is seen as a necessary ingredient of what is at stake.
>
> (McLaughlin, 1992, p. 356)

If we put together the requirements of what terrorism and extremism would entail in providing a historical and political contextual backdrop, along with the maximal interpretations of what a robust citizenship and political education that Callan and McLaughlin argue for, we begin to have a clearer directive in what should be emphasized in teaching about terrorism and extremism. This principle, however, should not necessarily be 'hostile to conservative political thought and policy' (*ibid.*, p. 237), but it requires that teachers attend to substantive issues related to identity, history, politics and culture.

Principle three: an examination of current inequitable circumstances is a necessary component in understanding extremism and terrorism

Thus far, I have articulated that basic content about terrorism and events such as 9/11 and 7/7 ought to be taught to students, particularly given that many will not recall the events. And further, such events ought to be addressed within the broader historical and political context which gives rise to them. The third principle, that of examining the socio-economic inequalities, is a prominent theme in understanding and potentially mitigating the threat of future terrorist attacks, emerging among prominent political theorists (i.e. Ramadan, 2008, 2010), economists (i.e. Sen, 2006) and counter-terrorist experts (i.e. Richardson, 2007). One must understand the broader inequitable economic and social conditions that fuel and give rise to extremist beliefs and acts of terrorism. Simply, 'the issue of fairness in a world of different groups and disparate identities demands a fuller understanding' (Sen, 2006, p. 134). We commonly skim over the debates that surround globalization and foreign policy directly and indirectly impacting the lives of millions in developing nations. Sen articulates a number of concerns that adversely affect many developing nations, including:

- the involvement of the world powers in the globalized trade in arms

- trade barriers that curb exports from the poorer countries
- inequitable patent laws, which can serve as counterproductive hurdles for the use of lifesaving drugs.

(ibid., pp. 139–41)

When economic and social conditions are such that they lead to a deprivation of one's primary needs in terms of food, shelter, education and medicine, such poverty inevitably leads to a sense of political helplessness. 'Injustice can feed discontent over a very long period … [and] the memory of destitution and devastation tends to linger, and can be invoked and utilized to generate rebellion and violence' *(ibid.*, p. 143). Even if one does not actively create policies that further inequitable conditions for individuals, being inactive or complicit in not taking action may also harbour resentment and violence. Long-term resentment, degradation and humiliation through abject poverty and poor living conditions become an easy recruiting ground for extremist groups.

In coming to understand the economic and social inequalities that may incite terrorist activity, we better understand the motives behind extremist groups. Richardson notes:

> If we do not even know what our enemies are fighting for, we cannot hope to counter them effectively. We have come to believe our own rhetoric that they are driven by uncontrolled evil and limitless ambition to harm us. We have tended to imagine all the terrible things they could do to us and then to attempt the impossible task of defending against all of them.
>
> (2006, pp. 209–10)

Now it may not necessarily be the task for us to deeply get inside the heads of terrorists per se, but if we are to develop students as future citizens able to engage and negotiate these complex issues of our times, we must then become attentive to such economic and social inequalities in a global context. And in coming to better understand 'the Other' beyond the superficial and rhetorical devices that reduce individuals, groups and nations to single identities, we challenge these narratives to offer a more nuanced perspective into the lives of individuals.

In doing this, we are not only looking out at the 'Other', but we become introspective. 'It is not possible to make simplistic conclusions about the "Other" without implicating the "Self"' (Kassam, 2010, p. 248). If we are to have a robust conception of what citizenship education entails, broadly speaking, we know that in order to 'play an effective role in public life' and learn 'to take part in decision-making and different forms of action' (DfE, 2011), a critical awareness of the inequitable economic and social conditions is a necessary component of understanding and attending to how these circumstances affect local and foreign policies.

Principle four: terrorism and extremism should be taught within a broader moral framework

This final principle offers a pedagogic recommendation for teachers regarding the extent to which they should remain neutral and allow open facilitation. In the previous chapter, I went into some depth regarding the political public values that should underpin the discussions about terrorism and extremism. I start with the premise that a moral directive is required when talking about terrorism and extremism. Allowing children to come to the conclusion that 'terrorism is morally acceptable' or, conversely, 'that all [fill in the blank] individuals are evil' is unhelpful, unproductive, and potentially damaging to the stability and social cohesion in civil society. And while some open facilitation may be a useful pedagogic endeavour in children working through the ideas, it is not a free-for-all where 'anything goes'. It is a delicate balance of children working through and processing their thoughts, perspectives and judgements in the process of developing the capacity of critical reasoning; it is another thing to allow children to say wilfully hateful sentiments that may marginalize or ostracize other members of their class.

> If the teacher will not act to protect students from gratuitous insult inside the classroom, those left unprotected are denied educational opportunity on fair terms. They are constrained from participating freely in the give and take of academic

discussion by the looming threat of verbal abuse from their peers, and when the abuse occurs, they cannot honourably withdraw from a humiliating situation without sacrificing their education.

(Callan, 2011, p. 6)

Clearly, such hostility was prevalent following 9/11 and 7/7 in classrooms directed toward particular students and teachers, as I have alluded throughout the book. In this case, Callan argues such verbal insult and attacks deprive the students of their educational opportunity on fair terms (*ibid.*, p. 6). Allowing for no interruption to hateful speech by the teacher furthers the racial or religious discrimination that one is trying to resist in the first place in trying to break down the societal contempt and stereotyping that occurs in various media. Open deliberation is compromised when uncivil speech occurs and those students who may be targeted in such discussions may feel impaired and reluctant to enter into such a discussion for fear of being further labelled.

A counter argument may be put forth that open speech provides a level of intellectual candour and is one of the underpinning principles within a 'democratic culture of free speech' (*ibid.*, p. 13). One might suggest that the way forward is not to curb such damaging or humiliating remarks, but to press the offending student to provide evidence and weigh the merits of such arguments. In this way, a moral directive is still prevalent in not allowing an 'anything goes' policy in the classroom, and the student is held accountable in justifying or becoming attentive to the way in which certain language may target particular individuals, and cause them harm, humiliation or embarrassment.

If there is a moral directive required in addressing terrorism and extremism, what are the main themes we should develop during these discussions? I wish to persuade educators that the common themes of patriotism and heroism in portraying the events of 9/11 may give a sense of pride and love of one's country, but they do not necessary offer much educational importance to how one understands and negotiates such events (Li and Brewer, 2004; Hand and Pearce, 2009; Merry, 2009; Jackson 2010). They remain 'thin' conceptions of citizenship that provide unreflective judgement and thought and instead play on the emotive, non-rational sentiments of why citizens should rally together.

In times of crisis or uncertainty, patriotism is commonly used in the citizenship curriculum as a rallying call for a renewed sense of love and civic obligation to one's country. And having a sense of national attachment provides solace and comfort, and a sense of being able to contribute to a more cohesive society. The problematic stance is when patriotism takes a militaristic turn, focusing on assimilationist education that excludes certain citizens within that nation state. Liz Jackson (2010) notes the intolerance of Muslims and Islam in public schools after 9/11 despite the fact that Muslims also contribute and participate as American citizens. Unfortunately, 'in wartime students are often presented with a narrow conception of civic virtue, most notably within the less formal aspects of their schooling, through the hidden curriculum or extracurricular activities and – with time – through the curriculum itself as well' (Ben-Porath, 2006, p. 38). Clearly, numerous examples exist that show this unreflective and unwavering support for patriotism:

> In October 2001, the Nebraska state board of education voted unanimously to endorse a 1949 state law that required school to teach lyrics to patriotic songs, reverence for the flag, and the dangers of communism. Officials at an elementary school in Rocklin, California, declined to remove a God Bless America sign after the American Civil Liberties Union complained that it violated the separation of church and state. Meanwhile, the U.S. House of Representatives gave its blessing to God Bless America, urging public schools to display the expression as a show of support for the nation. The nonbinding resolution passes, 404–0.
>
> (*ibid.*, p. 39)

The problematic aspect of putting such initiatives into place in schools is that it reduces the debate to that of a unifying, often assimilating stance, with little contextual backdrop. It further has the potential to ostracize and marginalize those individuals who feel they are already on the periphery of society.

In a similar vein, heroism creates a soothing sense of solidarity and a rise for one's sense of civic duty. And while it conjures up images of courage, strength and resilience, it detracts from the central debate about how to foster civic dispositions needed for a stable, cohesive society. Heroism creates a type of mythology that emphasizes the positives and silences the complexities.

> This notion of perpetual progress legitimizes ignoring anything bad America ever did, because in the end it turned out all right ... Unfortunately, this line of thinking disempowers students (and everyone else), for it implies that simply by working and living in society, American contribute to a nation that is constantly improving and remains the hope of the world.
>
> (Loewen, 2010, p. 78)

Again, it is not as if we can never talk about the heroes and the stories of hope that occurred in the terrorist attacks, but that should not be one of the primary aims. It reduces the complexity surrounding the events to the single narratives of human interest stories – that pull at the heartstrings and call for a love of one's country – but fails to address the historical, economic and political factors that give rise to such events. It further emphasizes the positive aspects with little attention to some of the negative factors that may have influenced the event. Little attention, for instance, is given to some of the lead up in lack of communication between various federal agencies, or the communication systems between the emergency response units between the police and fire departments. Instead, we focus on the firefighter who walked up the Twin Towers knowing that he would likely not escape. Heroism again whitewashes history and offers a narrow version of what occurred. 'Questioning the myths told in our textbooks is a first step toward good citizenship' (*ibid.*, p. 80).

Clearly, I will incite much opposition and perhaps hostility in suggesting the reduction of teaching patriotism and heroism when we discuss the issues of terrorism and extremism. Individuals may call me unpatriotic, a sympathizer of extremist fundamentalists or a person who undermines our very basic fundamental rights and freedoms. Yet what I call for is a more substantive understanding about the political dispositions required to address these issues in very real and robust ways.

Understanding the political structure from our society involves (although is perhaps not exclusive of):

1. understanding the underpinning principles that govern the rule of law (fundamental rights and freedoms);

2. understanding and applying how these fundamental principles affect both our rights as individuals and our obligations to our society;

3. understanding that despite individuals' fundamentally different religious, political, social and moral perspectives, one of the requirements of living in a pluralist society is to reconcile and live cohesively among individuals and groups.

Broadly speaking a moral directive is explicit, but governed by the public values upon which liberal democracies are founded.

Conclusion

Underpinning these four central principles are ten recommendations based on the discussions that have occurred throughout the book. One can sum up these recommendations as follows:

1. Reducing terrorist acts to single narratives and human interest stories does little to understand the circumstances that give rise to and follow up such an event.

2. Challenging the ways in which the media frame the discussion through rhetorical devices is an effective means for developing critical reflection and reasoned judgements in students.

3. Contesting and critically examining the way in which knowledge is constructed in society and used in creating a false dichotomy between 'us' and 'them' will help break down stereotypes and misunderstandings about individuals and groups.

4. Creating alternative dialogues and spaces for deliberation is helpful in allowing students to work through the complexity of events.

5. Open facilitation does not, however, mean that 'anything goes'.

6. A moral directive based upon the public political values should govern the nature of speech.

7. Understanding terrorism requires a self-reflection of how one's own society may incite greater resistance and hostility in potentially increasing extremist thoughts and terrorist activities both locally and abroad.

8. Understanding terrorism requires an examination of foreign policy that affect social and economic conditions in those countries that have incidences of extremist groups and terrorist activities.

9. The historical, economic, political and social conditions are essential components in assisting students to get a holistic picture of these issues.

10. Accountability for terrorists' actions need to be thought out with careful reasoned deliberation both in the short- and long-term.

I have elaborated on the first nine points throughout the book and will not spend time here reiterating the rationale behind these principles. The final point – point 10 – requires further elaboration. When an atrocity is committed it seems both justified and appropriate for the offending individual or group to be held accountable through legal judgement and punishment. I agree, as would most individuals. The contested aspect of this piece is the form of retribution that one might take to condemn the terrorist. How is it that we wish to emphasize this point with our students? Should the focus be on retribution, reconciliation or forgiveness? Can it be all three?

If we are to consider the first principle of understanding the underpinning principles that govern the political structure of civil society, then one of the considerations is the ways in which terrorist are brought to justice. Have the principles that guide our legal system been used in our accounts with suspected terrorists? How do we reconcile some of the practices that were used in bringing al-Qaida members to justice through the use of various interrogation techniques (such as waterboarding), or through conditions found at Guantanamo? If part of the educational task is for children to understand, exercise and respect the guiding principles that provide a stable and cohesive society, then a discussion might also be required about some of the ways countries undermine those principles in the name of preserving our freedom. Invasive phone tapping, heightened security measures, in the name of protecting one's freedoms, create an odd cognitive dissonance for teachers who wish to talk about responsible citizenship within the context of terrorism and extremism. One must model and abide by the underpinning fundamental rights and freedoms, if we are to expect others to come to respect and follow the same principles.

And in coming to understand and reduce the strength of terrorist cells, one might suggest discussions of what it might take to reduce the strength and resilience of these groups. Retribution may be a short-term goal in the hearts of citizens, but some consideration of long-term reconciliation may be required. It is through the eyes of two mothers that I mentioned in Chapter 2 – one of a victim of 9/11 and one of a man convicted of terrorism – that we might attempt to look beyond the local tragedy and examine the broader future implications. It is this aspect that is often neglected in moving forward, living among a diverse population of citizens, and coming to understand those we have previously feared. A long-term project might involve exploring the notion of political forgiveness within the citizenship curriculum (White, 2010).

It is clear that this book cannot resolve much of the contentious manner in which terrorism and extremism are taught in schools. I have attempted to argue for a robust teaching about terrorism and extremism that attends to the multi-causal factors that give rise to these fundamentalist beliefs and terrorist actions, rather than reducing it to single rhetorical narratives that conflate the issues and distract students. These guiding principles offer some consistency and justification for why certain emphases and value judgements about how to teach and what to teach about terrorism and extremism will be a bit clearer as you negotiate this issue within your local context and realities in your classroom.

Further reading

In trying to develop a set of guidelines and principles, I have found three complementary books that provide overlapping ideas in considering how one might address this in citizenship education. Sigal Ben-Porath's book, *Citizenship under Fire: Democratic education in times of conflict* (2006) speaks directly to some of the challenges that arise in teaching citizenship in times of long-term conflict and war. Lynn Davies' *Educating Against Extremism* (2008), offers some guiding principles within the parameters of free speech and offence, and the importance of humour and satire in addressing sensitive controversies. Finally, Linda Richardson's book, '*What Terrorists Want: Understanding the Enemy, Containing the Threat* (2007) provides a nuanced examination of the importance of understanding terrorist groups' motives and political and economic circumstances in reducing their platform's strength among their citizenry.

I conclude with a reflective book in how educators dealt with the events of 9/11 in very real ways. The book, *Forever After: New York City Teachers on 9/11* (Teachers College Press with Grolnick, 2006), brings together a collection of reflective pieces in how educators personally and professionally dealt with the event with their children in New York City.

REFERENCES

Agresto, J. (2002), 'Lessons of the Preamble', in Thomas Fordham Foundation (eds) *September 11: What our children need to know*, Washington DC: Thomas Fordham Foundation.

American Historical Association (1899) *The Study of History in Schools: Report by the Committee of Seven*. New York: Macmillan.

Andrews, M. (2000), 'Forgiveness in Context', *Journal of Moral Education*, 29(1), 75–86.

Andrews, R. and Mycock, A. (2008), 'Dilemmas of Devolution: The "politics of Britishness" and citizenship education', *British Politics*, 3, 139–55.

Associated Press (2007, February 28), 'Arizona bill would bar teachers from sharing political views in class'. Printed in First Amendment Center, Accessed 12 July 2011. www.firstamendmentcenter.org/ariz-bill-would-bar-teachers-from-sharing-political-views-in-class.

Barnes, L. P. (2002), 'Forgiveness, the moral law and education: A reply to Patricia White', *Journal of Philosophy of Education*, 36(4), 529–45.

Barrow, R., Gereluk, D. and Pring, R. (2008), 'Academic Freedom'. Invited panel symposium, Roehampton University, 9 April 2008.

Ben-Porath, S. (2006), *Citizenship under Fire: Democratic Education in Times of Conflict*, Princeton, NJ: Princeton University Press.

—(2007), 'Civic Virtue out of Necessity: Patriotism and Democratic Education', *Theory and Research in Education*, 5(1), 41–59.

—(forthcoming) 'Wartime Citizenship: An Argument for Shared Fate', *Ethnicities*.

Berberian, M. (2006), 'Hopeful visions: The faces of children', in Teachers College Press with Grolnick, M. (eds) *Forever After: New York City and the Teachers on 9/11*, New York: Teachers College Press.

Bernstein, B. (1970), 'Education cannot compensate for Society', *New Society*, 387, 344–7.

Bigelow, B. and Peterson, B. (2005), 'Terrorism and Globalization', *Whose Wars? Teaching about the Iraq War and the War on Terrorism*, Milwaukee: Rethinking Schools Collection.

Bin Laden, O. (2004) 'Message to America, October 30, 2004'.
    Translation in Lawrence, B. (ed.) *Messages to the World: The
    statements of Osama Bin Laden*, New York: Verso.
Blair, A. (2003) Speech to Foreign Office Conference: 'Britain in the
    world', London, 7 January.
Bowen, J. (2007) *Why the French Don't like Headscarves: Islam, the
    State and Public Space*, Princeton and Oxford: Princeton University
    Press.
Breslin, T., Rowe, D. and Thornton, A. (2006) *Citizenship Education:
    Current State of Play and Recommendations*, The Citizenship
    Foundation's written submission to the Education Select Committee
    (March) Accessed on 5 May 2011: www.citizenshipfoundation.org.uk/
    main/php? 280.
Breton, A., Galeotti, G., Salmon, P. and Wintrobe, W. (eds) (2002)
    Political Extremism and Rationality, Cambridge: Cambridge
    University Press.
Bridges, D. (1984) Non-paternalistic arguments in support of parents'
    rights over their children's education, *Journal of Philosophy of
    Education*, 18(1), 55–61.
—(2006) *Who's afraid of Children? Children, Conflict and International
    Relations*, Aldershot: Ashgate.
Brocklehurst, H. (2011) 'Education and the War on Terror: The early
    years', in Beier, J. ed. *The Militarization of Childhood: Thinking
    Beyond the Global*, Basingstoke: Palgrave Macmillan.
Brown, G. (2006) 'The Future of Britishness'. Speech made to the Fabian
    Society New Year Conference. Available at: www.fabians.org.uk/
    events/speeches/the-future-of-britishness. Accessed on 9 May 2011.
—(2007) Speech to a seminar on Britishness at the Commonwealth club
    London, 27 February 2007.
Callan, E. (1997) *Creating Citizens: Political Education and Liberal
    Democracy*, Oxford: Clarendon Press.
—(2006) 'Love, Idolatry and Patriotism', *Social Theory and Practice*,
    32(4) 525–46.
—(2011) 'When to shut students up: Civility, silencing, and free speech',
    Theory and Research in Education, 9(3), 3–22.
Cameron, D. (2007) 'Islam and Muslims in the World Today'. University
    of Cambridge. Available at: www.divinity.cam.ac.uk/cip/documents/
    DavidCameronSpeech2.pf. Accessed on 9 May 2011.
Carens, J. (2000) *Culture, Citizenship, and Community: A Contextual
    Exploration of Justice as Evenhandedness*, Oxford: Oxford University
    Press.
Carlisle, P. (2007) *One Day in History: September 11th*, New York:
    HarperCollins*Publishers*.

Carvalho, E. and Downing, D. (2010) *Academic Freedom in the Post-9/11 Era*, New York: Palgrave Macmillan.

Connolly, P. (2008) 'Retelling 9/11: How picture books re-envision national crises', *The Lion and the Unicorn*, 32(3), 288–303.

Corngold, J. (2011) 'Misplaced priorities: Gutmann's democratic theory, children's autonomy, and sex education policy', *Studies in Philosophy and Education*, 30(1), 67–84.

Curtiss, A. B. (2003) *The Little Chapel that Stood*, Escondido, CA: Oldcastle Publishing.

Davies, L. (2005) 'Schools and war: urgent agendas for comparative and international education, Compare: A Journal of Comparative and International Education', 35(4), 357–71.

Davies, L. (2008) *Educating against Extremism*, Stoke on Trent: Trentham Books.

Dearden, R. (1981) 'Controversial Issues and the Curriculum', in *Theory and Practice in Education*, London: Routledge and Kegan Paul.

Department for Education and Skills (2007) *Diversity and Citizenship Curriculum Review*, HM Government. Accessed on 21 July 2011. www.education.gov.uk/publications/.../DFES-00045-2007.

—(2008a) *Preventing Violent Extremism: A strategy for delivery*, HM Government, Accessed on 22 March 2010 http://publications.dcsf. gov.uk/eOrderingDownload/Preventing%20Violent%20Extremism. pdf.

Department for Children, Schools and Families (2008b) *Learning Together to be Safe: A toolkit to help schools contribute to the prevention of violent extremism*, Annesley, Nottingham: DCSF Publications. Accessed on 22 March 2010 (http://publications.dcsf. gov.uk/eOrderingDownload/00804-2008BKT-EN.pdf)

Department for Education (2003) *Racist Bullying: Listening to the views of children and young people*, Accessed on 12 July 2011. www. education.gov.uk/publications/standard/publicationDetail/Page1/ RB400.

—(2011) *Citizenship Key Stage three*, HM Government. Accessed on 22 July 2011. http://curriculum.qcda.gov.uk/key-stages-3-and-4/subjects/ key-stage-3/citizenship/index.aspx.

Dolch, A. (2006) 'By the way, this is not in the principal's manual', in Teachers College Press with Grolnick, M. (eds) *Forever After: New York City Teachers after 9/11*, New York: Teachers College Press.

Dworkin, R. (2002) 'Can there be a general theory of human rights?' Paul Sieghart Human Rights Memorial lecture Series, British Institute of Human Rights, 18 April 2002, London.

Edyvane, D. (2011) 'Britishness, Belonging and the Ideology of Conflict: Lessons from the polis', *Journal of Philosophy of Education*, 45(1), 75–94.

El Edroos, S. (2011) 'Learn to be Taliban – K is for Kalishnikov', *The Express Tribune*, accessed on 15 June 2011. http://blogs.tribune.com. pk/story/4877/learn-to-be-taliban-k-is-for-kalashinkov/.

English Current (2011) 'Terrorist Leader Osama Bin Laden Dead' (Intermediate News Lesson). A free website for English as a Second Language lesson plans. Accessed on 9 May 2011. www.englishcurrent. com/terrorist-leader-osama-bin-laden-dead-intermediate-news-lesson/.

Evans, R. (2004) *The Social Studies Wars: What should we teach the children?* New York: Teachers College Press.

Facing History and Ourselves (2011) 'Facing History and Ourselves: Linking the Past to the moral choices of today', Facing History Organization. www.facinghistory.org.

Fendler, L. (2001) 'Others and the problem of community', paper presented in Leuven, Belgium, Conference on Philosophy and History of the Discipline of Education: Evaluation and Evolution of the Criteria for Educational Research.

Finn, C. (2002) 'Introduction', in Thomas Fordham Foundation (eds) *September 11: What our children need to know*, Washington DC: Thomas Fordham Foundation.

Ganor, B. (2002) 'Defining Terrorism: Is one man's terrorist another man's freedom fighter?', *Police Practice and Research*, 3(4), 287–304.

Gereluk, D. (2006) *Education and Community*, London, New York: Continuum.

—(2009) 'Children's Autonomy and Symbolic Clothing in Schools: Help or hindrance?', in Yvonne Raley and Gerhard Preyer (eds) *Philosophy of Education in the Era of Globalization*, London, New York: Routledge.

—(2010) 'Should parents have a say in their children's schooling?' in Richard Bailey ed. *Introduction to Philosophy of Education*, London: Continuum.

Gereluk, D., Race, R. and Best, R. (2007) 'The Conference that dare not speak its name: Implications for the "War on Terror" in Education', Paper presented at the British Education Research Association Annual Meeting, London, 6 September 2007.

Gereluk, D. and Race, R. (2007) 'Multicultural Tensions in England, France and Canada: Contrasting approaches and consequences', *International Studies in Sociology of Education*, 17(1/ 2), 113–29.

Govier, T. (2002) *A Delicate Balance: What philosophy can tell us about terrorism*, Boulder, Colorado: Westview Press.

Grayling, A. C. (2009) *Liberty in the Age of Terror: A defence of civil liberties and enlightenment values*, London: Bloomsbury.

Gutmann, A. (2007) 'The lure and dangers of extremist rhetoric', *Doedalus*, 70–8.

Halstead, M. (1994) 'Muslim attitudes to music in schools', *British Journal of Music Education*, 11, 143–56.

—(1997) 'Muslims and Sex Education', *Journal of Moral Education*, 26(3), 317–30.

Hand, M. (2007) 'Should we teach homosexuality as a controversial issue?' *Theory and Research in Education*, 5(1) 69–86.

—(2008) 'What should we teach as controversial? A defense of the epistemic criterion', *Educational Theory*, 58(2), 213–28.

—(2010) 'Moral education and the idea of reasonable moral pluralism', Keynote paper presented at the Philosophy of Education Society of Great Britain Annual Meeting, 28 March 2010.

Hand, M. and Pearce, J. (2007) 'Patriotism in British Schools, Principles, practices and press hysteria', *Educational Philosophy and Theory*, 41(4), 453–65.

Hand, M., Gereluk, D. Hayward, J., McAvoy, P. and Warnick, B. (2010) 'What schools are scared to teach: addressing sensitive controversies in the classroom', panel symposium, Philosophy of Education Annual Meeting, San Francisco, 11 April 2010.

Haw, K. (2009) 'From hijab to jilbab and the "myth" of British identity: Being Muslim in contemporary Britain a half-generation on', *Race, Ethnicity and Education*, 12(3) 363–78.

—(2010) 'Being, Becoming and Belonging: Young Muslim Women in Contemporary Britain', *Journal of Intercultural Studies*, 31(4), 345–61.

Herbert, I. (2007) 'Veils block integration in UK, learns Lord Ahmed'. *The Independent*, 21 February.

Hess, D. (2009) *Controversy in the Classroom: The democratic power of discussion*, New York: Routledge.

Hess, D., McAvoy, P., Smithson, J. and Hwang, H. (2008) 'The nature, range, and impact of ideological diversity and teacher disclosure in high school democratic education courses'. Paper presented at the American Educational Research Association Annual Meeting, New York,.

Hess, D. and Stoddard, J. (2007) '9/11 and terrorism: "The ultimate teachable moment" in textbooks and supplemental curricula', *Social Education*, 71(5), 231–6.

Hoff, D. (11 September 2002) 'A Year Later: Impact of 9/11 Still Lingers', *Education Week*, 22(2), 1–3.

Jackson, L. (2010) 'The New Assimilation: The push for "patriotic" education in the United States Since September 11', *Journal for Critical Education Policy Studies*, 8(1), 109–36.

Johnson, A. (2007) 'Schools "Must Teach Britishness"'. BBC. Available at: http://news/bbc/cok.uk/1/hi/education/6294643.stm. Accessed on 9 May 2011.

Kalma, M. (2002) *Fireboat: The Heroic Adventures of the John J. Harvey*, New York: G. P. Putnam's Sons-Penguin.

Kassam, K. (2010) *Understanding Terror: Perspectives for Canadians*, Calgary, AB: University of Calgary Press.

Kymlicka, W. (1989) *Liberalism, Community and Culture*, Oxford: Oxford University Press.

—(1995) *Multicultural Citizenship: A liberal Theory of Minority Rights*, Oxford: Oxford University Press.

Lantieri, L. with Nambiar, M. and Chavez-Reilly, C. (2006) 'Building inner preparedness', in Teachers College Press with Grolnick, M. (eds) *Forever After: New York City and the Teachers on 9/11*, New York: Teachers College Press.

Laqueur, W. (1977, 2009) *The History of Terrorism*, New Jersey: Transaction Publishers.

—(1987) *The Age of Terrorism*, Boston, Toronto: Little, Brown and Company.

Law, R. (2009) *Terrorism: A History*, Cambridge, MA: Polity Press.

Leahey, C. (2009) *Whitewashing War: Historical Myth, Corporate Textbooks, and Possibilities for Democratic Education*, New York: Teachers College Press.

Lengua, L., Long, A., Smith, K. and Meltzoff, A. (2005) 'Pre-attack symptomatology and temperament as predictors of children's responses to the September 11 terrorist attacks', *Journal of Child Psychology and Psychiatry*, 46(6), 631–45.

Lent, P. (2002) 'Moving back and moving on', in Teachers College Press with Grolnick, M. (eds) *Forever After: New York City Teachers on 9/11*, New York: Teachers College Press.

Li, Q. and Brewer, M. (2004) 'What does it mean to be an American? Patriotism, nationalism and American identity after 9/11', *Political Psychology*, 25(5), 727–39.

Lipsett, A. (2009) 'Teaching pack about 7/7 bombers withdrawn: pupils were invited to imagine themselves from the perspective of the bombers', *The Guardian*, 20 February 2009, accessed on 18 August 2011. www.guardian.co.uk/education/2009/feb/20/bombers-pack-withdrawn.

Loewen, J. (2009) *Teaching What Really Happened: How to avoid the tyranny of textbooks and get students excited about doing history*, New York: Teachers College Press.

McKinnley Jr, Ken (10 March 2010) 'Texas Conservatives win Curriculum Change', *New York Times*, accessed on 4 May 2011. www.nytimes.com/2010/03/13/education/13texas.html.

McLaughlin, T. (1984) 'Parental rights and the religious upbringing of children', *Journal of Philosophy of Education*, 18(1), 75–83.

—(1992) 'Citizenship, Diversity and Education: A philosophical perspective', *Journal of Moral Education*, 21(3), 235–50.

—(1994) 'Values, coherence and the school', *Cambridge Journal of Education*, 24(3), 453–71.

Mansell, W, Milne, J., Barker, I., Shaw, M. and Bloom, A. (18 April 2008) 'Terrorism and action moves for new GCSE'. *Times Educational Supplement*, No 4784.

Maylor, U. and Read, B. (2007) *Diversity and Citizenship in the Curriculum: Research Review*, London: Department for Education and Skills.

Melnyk, G. (2010) 'The Word "Terrorism" and its Impact on Public Consciousness', in Kassam, K. ed. *Understanding Terror: Perspectives for Canadians*, Calgary, AB: University of Calgary Press.

Merry, M. (2007) *Culture, Identity, and Islamic Schooling: A philosophical approach*, New York and Houndmills, Basingstoke: Palgrave Macmillan.

—(2009) 'Patriotism, History and the Legitimate Aims of American Education', *Educational Philosophy and Theory*, 41(4), 368–98.

Miller, R. (2007) 'Unlearning American Patriotism', *Theory and Research in Education*, 5(1), 7–22.

Moller-Okin, S. (1999) *Is Multiculturalism Bad for Women?*, ed. by J. Cohen, M. Howard and M. Nussbaum. Princeton, NJ: Princeton University Press.

Morton, A. (2004) *On Evil*, London: Routledge.

Nussbaum, M. (2003) 'The complexity of groups', *Philosophy and Social Affairs*, 29(1), 57–70.

Orwell, G. (1949). *Nineteen Eighty-Four*. New York: Harcourt, Brace & Co.

Patel, A. (2002) *On that Day: A book of Hope for Children*, Berkeley: Tricycle Publishers.

PBS (2010) 'America Responds: Addressing September 11, 2001'. Accessed on 30 March 2010. www.pbs.org/americaresponds/educators.html.

Phillips, T. (2004) Civil service race equality network annual lecture, 26 April 2004. London, Commission for Racial Equality.

—(2005) 'After 7/7: sleepwalking to segregation', speech given at the Commission for Racial Equality, 22 September. London, Commission for Racial Equality.

Pinsky, D. (2011) 'Our Children: Understanding terrorism', CNN broadcast, Aired 3 May 2011. Accessed on 9 May 2011. http://edition.cnn.com/TRANSCRIPTS/1105/03/ddhln.01.html.

Ramadan, T. (2008) *Radical Reform, Islamic Ethics and Liberation*, Oxford: Oxford University Press.

—(2009) *The Quest for Meaning: Developing a Philosophy of Pluralism,* London: Penguin.

—(2010) 'Good Muslim, Bad Muslim'. Accessed 21 July 2011. www. tariqramadan.com/Good-Muslim-Bad-Muslim.html.

Rawls, J. (1971) *A Theory of Justice,* Oxford: Oxford University Press.

—(1985) 'Justice as fairness: political not metaphysical', *Philosophy and Public Affairs,* 14(3), 223–51.

—(1996) *Political Liberalism* (expanded version), New York: Columbia University Press.

—(2001) *Justice as Fairness: A Restatement,* ed. Erin Kelly, London: Belknap Press of Harvard University Press.

Reich, R. (2002). 'Opting out of education: Yoder, Mozert and the autonomy of children', *Educational Theory,* 52(4), 445–62.

Rethinking Schools (2001), *War, Terrorism and our Classrooms: Teaching in the Aftermath of the September 11th Tragedy.* Accessed on 16 March 2010. www.rethinkingschools.org/special_reports/sept11/ pdf/911insrt.pdf.

Rex, J. and Moore, R. (1969) *Race, Community and Conflict: Study of Sparkbrook,* Oxford: Oxford University Press.

Richardson, J. (2001) 'British Muslims in the Broadsheet Press: a challenge to cultural hegemony?', *Journalism Studies,* 2(2), 221–42.

—(2004) *(Mis)Representing Islam: The racism and rhetoric of British Broadsheet newspapers.* Amsterdam: John Benjamins Publishers.

Richardson, L. (2007) *What Terrorists Want: Understanding the Enemy, Containing the Threat,* New York: Random House.

Richardson, R. (2009) 'Islamophobia or Anti-Muslim Racism – or what? – concepts and terms revisited', Paper presented at University of Birmingham, 9 December 2009.

Risinger, C. F. (2001) 'Reflections in a Time of Crisis: Teaching about Terrorism, Islam, and tolerance with the Internet', *Social Education,* 65 (7), 426–7.

Romanowski, M. (2009) 'What you don't know can hurt you: textbook omissions and 9/11', *The Clearing House,* 82, 6.

Rose, N. (1999) *Powers of Freedom: Reframing Political Thought,* Cambridge: Cambridge University Press.

Said, E. (1993) *Culture and Imperialism,* London: Vintage.

Sawyer, C. (2011) 'One: A 9-11 Remembrance Ceremony', *9/11 National Day of Service and Remembrance,* a website for free lesson plans on 9/11. Accessed on 19 May 2011. http://home.roadrunner.com/~scoutin gseasons/9patriotday.htm.

Scott, M. (2008) 'Considering Terrorism: What is terrorism? What are "terrorists" trying to achieve? Are they achieving it? At what cost?'

Association of Citizenship Teaching, Accessed on 22 March 2010. www.teachingcitizenship.org.uk/theme?t=18.

Silberstein, S. (2002) *War of Words: Language, Politics and 9/11,* London: Routledge.

Smith, A. (2005) 'Education in the twenty-first century: Conflict, reconstruction and reconciliation', *Compare: A Journal of Comparative and International Education,* 35(4), 373–91.

Sparrow, A. (2011) 'England riots: Cameron and Miliband speeches and reaction – August 15, 2011', *The Guardian,* accessed on 16 August 2011. www.guardian.co.uk/politics/blog/2011/aug/15/england-riots-cameron-miliband-speeches#block-46.

Taylor, C. (1994) *Multiculturalism: Examining the politics of recognition,* edited by Amy Gutmann, Princeton NJ: Princeton University Press.

Teachers College Press with Grolnick, M. (eds) *Forever After: New York City Teachers on 9/11,* New York and London: Teachers College Press.

Thobani, S. (2010) *Islam in the School Curriculum: Symbolic Pedagogy and Cultural Claims,* London, New York: Continuum.

Thomas Fordham Foundation (eds) (2002) *September 11: What our children need to know,* Washington DC: Thomas Fordham Foundation.

Tutu, D. (1999) *No Future without Forgiveness,* London: Rider.

Walzer, M. (1983) *Spheres of Justice: A defence of pluralism and equality,* New York: Basic Books.

Ward, L. (2007) 'From Aladdin to Lost Ark, Muslims get angry at "bad guy" film images: Crude and exaggerated stereotypes are fuelling Islamophobia, says study', *The Guardian,* 25 January 2007. Accessed on 4 July 2011. www.guardian.co.uk/media/2007/jan/25/broadcasting.race.

Werbner, P. (2005) 'Islamophobia: Incitement to religious hatred-legislating a new fear', *Anthropology Today,* 21(1) 5–9.

White, P. (2002) 'What should we teach children about forgiveness?', *Journal of Philosophy of Education,* 36(1), 57–67.

—(2007) 'Political Forgiveness and Citizenship Education', in Rita Casale and Rebekka Horlacher (eds) *Bildung und Öffentlichkeit, Weinheim und Basel,* Beltz Verlag.

—(2011) 'Does a democracy need angry citizens?' Keynote address presented at the Annual Meeting of the Philosophy of Education Society in Great Britain, Oxford, 1 April 2011.

White, R. Wyn, J. and Albanese, P. (2011) *Youth & Society: Exploring the social dynamics of youth experience,* Oxford: Oxford University Press.

Win, J. (2009) *Youth Health and Welfare: The Culture Politics of Education and Wellbeing,* Oxford: Oxford University Press.

Wingo, A. (2007) 'To Love Your Country as Your Mother: Patriotism after 9/11', *Theory and Research in Education*, 5(1), 23–40.

Winter, J. (2004) 'September Roses', *Bulletin of the Center of Children's Book*, 58(1), 45–6.

Young, I. M. (2000) *Inclusion and Democracy*, Oxford: Oxford University Press.

Zaraboz, J. (2003) 'The Concepts of "Extremism" and "Terrorism"', *Journal of Islamic Law and Culture*, 8(2), 50–67.

Zinn, H. (2004) 'The Optimism of Uncertainty', *The Nation*, 2 September 2004. Accessed on 16 August 2011. www.thenation.com/article/optimism-uncertainty.

INDEX